Propensity Score Methods and Applications

Propensity Score Methods and Applications

Haiyan Bai

University of Central Florida

M. H. Clark

University of Central Florida

Los Angeles | London | New Delhi
Singapore | Washington DC | Melbourne

Quantitative Applications in the Social Sciences

A SAGE PUBLICATIONS SERIES

1. **Analysis of Variance, 2nd Edition** *Iversen/ Norpoth*
2. **Operations Research Methods** *Nagel/Neef*
3. **Causal Modeling, 2nd Edition** *Asher*
4. **Tests of Significance** *Henkel*
5. **Cohort Analysis, 2nd Edition** *Glenn*
6. **Canonical Analysis and Factor Comparison** *Levine*
7. **Analysis of Nominal Data, 2nd Edition** *Reynolds*
8. **Analysis of Ordinal Data** *Hildebrand/Laing/ Rosenthal*
9. **Time Series Analysis, 2nd Edition** *Ostrom*
10. **Ecological Inference** *Langbein/Lichtman*
11. **Multidimensional Scaling** *Kruskal/Wish*
12. **Analysis of Covariance** *Wildt/Ahtola*
13. **Introduction to Factor Analysis** *Kim/Mueller*
14. **Factor Analysis** *Kim/Mueller*
15. **Multiple Indicators** *Sullivan/Feldman*
16. **Exploratory Data Analysis** *Hartwig/Dearing*
17. **Reliability and Validity Assessment** *Carmines/Zeller*
18. **Analyzing Panel Data** *Markus*
19. **Discriminant Analysis** *Klecka*
20. **Log-Linear Models** *Knoke/Burke*
21. **Interrupted Time Series Analysis** *McDowall/ McCleary/Meidinger/Hay*
22. **Applied Regression, 2nd Edition** *Lewis-Beck/ Lewis-Beck*
23. **Research Designs** *Spector*
24. **Unidimensional Scaling** *McIver/Carmines*
25. **Magnitude Scaling** *Lodge*
26. **Multiattribute Evaluation** *Edwards/Newman*
27. **Dynamic Modeling** *Huckfeldt/Kohfeld/Likens*
28. **Network Analysis** *Knoke/Kuklinski*
29. **Interpreting and Using Regression** *Achen*
30. **Test Item Bias** *Osterlind*
31. **Mobility Tables** *Hout*
32. **Measures of Association** *Liebetrau*
33. **Confirmatory Factor Analysis** *Long*
34. **Covariance Structure Models** *Long*
35. **Introduction to Survey Sampling** *Kalton*
36. **Achievement Testing** *Bejar*
37. **Nonrecursive Causal Models** *Berry*
38. **Matrix Algebra** *Namboodiri*
39. **Introduction to Applied Demography** *Rives/Serow*
40. **Microcomputer Methods for Social Scientists, 2nd Edition** *Schrodt*
41. **Game Theory** *Zagare*
42. **Using Published Data** *Jacob*
43. **Bayesian Statistical Inference** *Iversen*
44. **Cluster Analysis** *Aldenderfer/Blashfield*
45. **Linear Probability, Logit, and Probit Models** *Aldrich/Nelson*
46. **Event History and Survival Analysis, 2nd Edition** *Allison*
47. **Canonical Correlation Analysis** *Thompson*
48. **Models for Innovation Diffusion** *Mahajan/Peterson*
49. **Basic Content Analysis, 2nd Edition** *Weber*
50. **Multiple Regression in Practice** *Berry/Feldman*
51. **Stochastic Parameter Regression Models** *Newbold/Bos*
52. **Using Microcomputers in Research** *Madron/Tate/Brookshire*
53. **Secondary Analysis of Survey Data** *Kiecolt/ Nathan*
54. **Multivariate Analysis of Variance** *Bray/ Maxwell*
55. **The Logic of Causal Order** *Davis*
56. **Introduction to Linear Goal Programming** *Ignizio*
57. **Understanding Regression Analysis, 2nd Edition** *Schroeder/Sjoquist/Stephan*
58. **Randomized Response and Related Methods, 2nd Edition** *Fox/Tracy*
59. **Meta-Analysis** *Wolf*
60. **Linear Programming** *Feiring*
61. **Multiple Comparisons** *Klockars/Sax*
62. **Information Theory** *Krippendorff*
63. **Survey Questions** *Converse/Presser*
64. **Latent Class Analysis** *McCutcheon*
65. **Three-Way Scaling and Clustering** *Arabie/ Carroll/DeSarbo*
66. **Q Methodology, 2nd Edition** *McKeown/ Thomas*
67. **Analyzing Decision Making** *Louviere*
68. **Rasch Models for Measurement** *Andrich*
69. **Principal Components Analysis** *Dunteman*
70. **Pooled Time Series Analysis** *Sayrs*
71. **Analyzing Complex Survey Data, 2nd Edition** *Lee/Forthofer*
72. **Interaction Effects in Multiple Regression, 2nd Edition** *Jaccard/Turrisi*
73. **Understanding Significance Testing** *Mohr*
74. **Experimental Design and Analysis** *Brown/Melamed*
75. **Metric Scaling** *Weller/Romney*
76. **Longitudinal Research, 2nd Edition** *Menard*
77. **Expert Systems** *Benfer/Brent/Furbee*
78. **Data Theory and Dimensional Analysis** *Jacoby*
79. **Regression Diagnostics** *Fox*
80. **Computer-Assisted Interviewing** *Saris*
81. **Contextual Analysis** *Iversen*
82. **Summated Rating Scale Construction** *Spector*
83. **Central Tendency and Variability** *Weisberg*
84. **ANOVA: Repeated Measures** *Girden*
85. **Processing Data** *Bourque/Clark*
86. **Logit Modeling** *DeMaris*
87. **Analytic Mapping and Geographic Databases** *Garson/Biggs*
88. **Working With Archival Data** *Elder/Pavalko/Clipp*
89. **Multiple Comparison Procedures** *Toothaker*
90. **Nonparametric Statistics** *Gibbons*
91. **Nonparametric Measures of Association** *Gibbons*
92. **Understanding Regression Assumptions** *Berry*
93. **Regression With Dummy Variables** *Hardy*
94. **Loglinear Models With Latent Variables** *Hagenaars*
95. **Bootstrapping** *Mooney/Duval*
96. **Maximum Likelihood Estimation** *Eliason*
97. **Ordinal Log-Linear Models** *Ishii-Kuntz*
98. **Random Factors in ANOVA** *Jackson/Brashers*
99. **Univariate Tests for Time Series Models** *Cromwell/Labys/Terraza*
100. **Multivariate Tests for Time Series Models** *Cromwell/Hannan/Labys/Terraza*

Quantitative Applications in the Social Sciences

A SAGE PUBLICATIONS SERIES

101. **Interpreting Probability Models: Logit, Probit, and Other Generalized Linear Models** Liao
102. **Typologies and Taxonomies** Bailey
103. **Data Analysis: An Introduction** Lewis-Beck
104. **Multiple Attribute Decision Making** Yoon/Hwang
105. **Causal Analysis With Panel Data** Finkel
106. **Applied Logistic Regression Analysis, 2nd Edition** Menard
107. **Chaos and Catastrophe Theories** Brown
108. **Basic Math for Social Scientists: Concepts** Hagle
109. **Basic Math for Social Scientists: Problems and Solutions** Hagle
110. **Calculus** Iversen
111. **Regression Models: Censored, Sample Selected, or Truncated Data** Breen
112. **Tree Models of Similarity and Association** James E. Corter
113. **Computational Modeling** Taber/Timpone
114. **LISREL Approaches to Interaction Effects in Multiple Regression** Jaccard/Wan
115. **Analyzing Repeated Surveys** Firebaugh
116. **Monte Carlo Simulation** Mooney
117. **Statistical Graphics for Univariate and Bivariate Data** Jacoby
118. **Interaction Effects in Factorial Analysis of Variance** Jaccard
119. **Odds Ratios in the Analysis of Contingency Tables** Rudas
120. **Statistical Graphics for Visualizing Multivariate Data** Jacoby
121. **Applied Correspondence Analysis** Clausen
122. **Game Theory Topics** Fink/Gates/Humes
123. **Social Choice: Theory and Research** Johnson
124. **Neural Networks** Abdi/Valentin/Edelman
125. **Relating Statistics and Experimental Design: An Introduction** Levin
126. **Latent Class Scaling Analysis** Dayton
127. **Sorting Data: Collection and Analysis** Coxon
128. **Analyzing Documentary Accounts** Hodson
129. **Effect Size for ANOVA Designs** Cortina/Nouri
130. **Nonparametric Simple Regression: Smoothing Scatterplots** Fox
131. **Multiple and Generalized Nonparametric Regression** Fox
132. **Logistic Regression: A Primer** Pampel
133. **Translating Questionnaires and Other Research Instruments: Problems and Solutions** Behling/Law
134. **Generalized Linear Models: A Unified Approach** Gill
135. **Interaction Effects in Logistic Regression** Jaccard
136. **Missing Data** Allison
137. **Spline Regression Models** Marsh/Cormier
138. **Logit and Probit: Ordered and Multinomial Models** Borooah
139. **Correlation: Parametric and Nonparametric Measures** Chen/Popovich
140. **Confidence Intervals** Smithson
141. **Internet Data Collection** Best/Krueger
142. **Probability Theory** Rudas
143. **Multilevel Modeling** Luke
144. **Polytomous Item Response Theory Models** Ostini/Nering
145. **An Introduction to Generalized Linear Models** Dunteman/Ho
146. **Logistic Regression Models for Ordinal Response Variables** O'Connell
147. **Fuzzy Set Theory: Applications in the Social Sciences** Smithson/Verkuilen
148. **Multiple Time Series Models** Brandt/Williams
149. **Quantile Regression** Hao/Naiman
150. **Differential Equations: A Modeling Approach** Brown
151. **Graph Algebra: Mathematical Modeling With a Systems Approach** Brown
152. **Modern Methods for Robust Regression** Andersen
153. **Agent-Based Models** Gilbert
154. **Social Network Analysis, 2nd Edition** Knoke/Yang
155. **Spatial Regression Models, 2nd Edition** Ward/Gleditsch
156. **Mediation Analysis** Iacobucci
157. **Latent Growth Curve Modeling** Preacher/Wichman/MacCallum/Briggs
158. **Introduction to the Comparative Method With Boolean Algebra** Caramani
159. **A Mathematical Primer for Social Statistics** Fox
160. **Fixed Effects Regression Models** Allison
161. **Differential Item Functioning, 2nd Edition** Osterlind/Everson
162. **Quantitative Narrative Analysis** Franzosi
163. **Multiple Correspondence Analysis** LeRoux/Rouanet
164. **Association Models** Wong
165. **Fractal Analysis** Brown/Liebovitch
166. **Assessing Inequality** Hao/Naiman
167. **Graphical Models and the Multigraph Representation for Categorical Data** Khamis
168. **Nonrecursive Models** Paxton/Hipp/Marquart-Pyatt
169. **Ordinal Item Response Theory** Van Schuur
170. **Multivariate General Linear Models** Haase
171. **Methods of Randomization in Experimental Design** Alferes
172. **Heteroskedasticity in Regression** Kaufman
173. **An Introduction to Exponential Random Graph Modeling** Harris
174. **Introduction to Time Series Analysis** Pickup
175. **Factorial Survey Experiments** Auspurg/Hinz
176. **Introduction to Power Analysis: Two-Group Studies** Hedberg
177. **Linear Regression: A Mathematical Introduction** Gujarati
178. **Propensity Score Methods and Applications** Bai/Clark

FOR INFORMATION:

SAGE Publications, Inc.
2455 Teller Road
Thousand Oaks, California 91320
E-mail: order@sagepub.com

SAGE Publications Ltd.
1 Oliver's Yard
55 City Road
London EC1Y 1SP
United Kingdom

SAGE Publications India Pvt. Ltd.
B 1/I 1 Mohan Cooperative Industrial Area
Mathura Road, New Delhi 110 044
India

SAGE Publications Asia-Pacific Pte. Ltd.
18 Cross Street #10-10/11/12
China Square Central
Singapore 048423

Acquisitions Editor: Helen Salmon
Editorial Assistant: Megan O'Heffernan
Content Development Editor: Chelsea Neve
Production Editor: Astha Jaiswal
Copy Editor: Liann Lech
Typesetter: C&M Digitals (P) Ltd.
Proofreader: Scott Oney
Indexer: Will Ragsdale
Cover Designer: Candice Harman
Marketing Manager: Susannah Goldes

Copyright © 2019 by SAGE Publications, Inc.

All rights reserved. No part of this book may be reproduced or utilized in any form or by any means, electronic or mechanical, including photocopying, recording, or by any information storage and retrieval system, without permission in writing from the publisher.

Printed in the United States of America

ISBN: 9781506378053

This book is printed on acid-free paper.

18 19 20 21 22 10 9 8 7 6 5 4 3 2 1

CONTENTS

Series Editor's Introduction	ix
About the Authors	xi
Acknowledgments	xiii

1. **Basic Concepts of Propensity Score Methods** — 1
   - 1.1 Causal Inference — 3
   - 1.2 Propensity Scores — 9
   - 1.3 Assumptions — 13
   - 1.4 Summary of the Chapter — 19

2. **Covariate Selection and Propensity Score Estimation** — 21
   - 2.1 Covariate Selection — 21
   - 2.2 Propensity Score Estimation — 26
   - 2.3 Summary of the Chapter — 31
   - 2.4 An Example — 31

3. **Propensity Score Adjustment Methods** — 39
   - 3.1 Propensity Score Matching — 39
   - 3.2 Other Propensity Score Adjustment Methods — 49
   - 3.3 Summary of the Chapter — 57
   - 3.4 An Example — 58

4. **Covariate Evaluation and Causal Effect Estimation** — 65
   - 4.1 Evaluating the Balance of Covariate Distributions — 65
   - 4.2 Causal Effect Estimation — 71
   - 4.3 Sensitivity Analysis — 77
   - 4.4 Summary of the Chapter — 79
   - 4.5 An Example — 80

5. **Conclusion** — 89
   - 5.1 Limitations of the Propensity Score Methods and How to Address Them — 89
   - 5.2 Summary of Propensity Score Procedures — 92
   - 5.3 Final Comments — 99

References — 105
Index — 113

SERIES EDITOR'S INTRODUCTION

Considering the QASS volumes as a whole, there is a topic that is notably missing: Propensity Score Methods. Thus, it is with particular pleasure that I introduce a volume designed to fill this gap, *Propensity Score Methods and Applications*, by Haiyan Bai and M. H. Clark.

In most applications, including many interventions of interest to basic as well as applied social scientists, random assignment is an ideal rather than a reality. For ethical and/or practical reasons, it is not possible to assign participants to treatment and control groups. Treatment and control groups may differ in ways that matter for estimating the causal effect of interest. Propensity score methods help balance non-equivalent groups by estimating the likelihood that individuals are assigned to or self-select into the treatment group and using this information to make design-based adjustments to the analysis. *Propensity Score Methods and Applications* explains the theory behind and the methodology underlying these techniques.

The volume is broadly accessible and well organized, flows logically, offers clear explanations, and provides much practical advice. Indeed, the authors are experienced teachers of propensity score methods as well as contributors to the published literature on applications of these methods. The focus throughout is the estimation of a causal effect, especially one tied to an intervention of some sort, in the face of selection bias. The volume introduces propensity scores and reviews assumptions underlying their use (Chapter 1), explains the modeling and evaluation of propensity scores (Chapter 2), provides a review of common propensity score methods (matching, subclassification, inverse probability weighting, covariate adjustment) and reasons for choosing one rather than another (Chapter 3), discusses issues that arise in application including assessment of individual covariates for balance across groups and estimation of adjusted treatment effects (Chapter 4), and concludes with a summary, a discussion of limitations, and pointers to new developments (Chapter 5). The text includes simple examples based on a handful of cases and also develops a more extended application based on a subset of data from the Playworks intervention, a recess program for elementary school children. Readers can test their understanding by replicating the results shown in the text using the Playworks data as well as instructions in R, SPSS, SAS, and STATA available in a companion website at **study.sagepub.com/researchmethods/qass/bai&clark**.

Propensity Score Methods and Applications offers a helpful hands-on introduction to readers interested in learning about propensity score methods, laying a foundation for the more technical literature. It can serve as a useful supplement in a graduate-level methods or statistics class in any number of disciplines, including political science, sociology, or education. It works equally well as a stand-alone tutorial for researchers no longer taking formal classes. Enjoy!

Barbara Entwisle
Series Editor

ABOUT THE AUTHORS

Haiyan Bai is a professor at the University of Central Florida. She earned her PhD in quantitative research methodology at the University of Cincinnati. Her research interests include issues that revolve around statistical/quantitative methods, specifically propensity score methods, resampling techniques, research design, measurement, and the application of statistical methods in social and behavioral sciences.

M. H. Clark is an associate lecturer, statistical consultant, and program evaluator at the University of Central Florida. She has a PhD in experimental psychology with a specialization in research design and statistics from the University of Memphis. Her specific areas of expertise are in causal inference, selection bias in nonrandomized experiments, and propensity score methods.

ACKNOWLEDGMENTS

We would like to thank the editors of this book, and the following reviewers, for their feedback and encouragement:

Adam Seth Litwin, Cornell University

Christopher M. Sedelmaier, University of New Haven

Kenneth Elpus, University of Maryland

Cherng-Jyh Yen, Old Dominion University

Mido Chang, Florida International University

We dedicate this book to our families, especially Wei Guo and Pete Mellen, for their great support.

CHAPTER 1. BASIC CONCEPTS OF PROPENSITY SCORE METHODS

In behavioral and social sciences, due to practical or ethical barriers, researchers often cannot collect data from random trials (Bai, 2011). Therefore, observational studies are often used to make causal inferences (Pan & Bai, 2015a; Shadish, Cook, & Campbell, 2002). Unfortunately, selection bias in observational research often poses a threat to the validity of these studies (Rosenbaum & Rubin, 1983). Selection bias occurs when the participants in one study condition (e.g., the treatment group) are systematically different in their preexisting characteristics from those in another condition (e.g., the control group). For example, if participants self-select into a treatment group, they may be more motivated, more conscientious, or more ambitious than those in the control group. When participants are randomly assigned to groups, this bias is usually reduced. On expectation, participants who are randomly assigned will have similar distributions of characteristics between the groups (i.e., those in the control group are just as motivated, conscientious, and ambitious as those in the treatment group). When covariates are equivalent across groups, they are balanced, and researchers can reasonably infer that any differences between the groups on the outcome variable are due to the causal (predictor or independent) variable. If covariates are not balanced, as is often the case in observation studies, the preexisting differences between the groups may be responsible for any differences that we see in the outcome variables, resulting in a spurious treatment effect. To increase the validity of the treatment effect estimation, a variety of statistical adjustments may be used to reduce selection bias; however, some are more effective than others.

Over the past decades, propensity score (PS) methods have become increasingly popular for improving the validity of causal studies, as they can produce results that mimic those from true experimental designs when used appropriately (Rosenbaum & Rubin, 1985). Since their introduction by Rosenbaum and Rubin in 1983, PS methods have been used in many fields, such as education (e.g., Clark & Cundiff, 2011; Guill, Lüdtke, & Köller, 2017; Hong & Raudenbush, 2005), epidemiology (e.g., Austin, 2009; Thanh & Rapoport, 2016), psychology (e.g., Gunter & Daly, 2012; Kirchmann et al., 2012), economics (e.g., Baycan, 2016; Dehejia & Wahba, 2002), political science (Seawright & Gerring, 2008), and program evaluation (e.g., Duwe, 2015). For example, Gunter and Daly used propensity scores when examining the relationship between violent video games and deviant behavior. They found that after accounting for self-selection of the type of games played, PS matching decreased the treatment estimates, indicating that video games have a weaker effect on violent and deviant behaviors than previous research had suggested. Guill et al. compared several PS models to account for selection bias when examining how students on an academic track differed from those either on a nonacademic track or attending a comprehensive school on cognitive development. Duwe used PS matching to evaluate how well a prisoner reentry program reduced recidivism and increased postrelease employment.

Although research across a variety of fields has demonstrated that PS methods consistently improve the accuracy of treatment effects, there are still some challenges for researchers who apply these methods to their own empirical studies (Pan & Bai, 2016). While there are other volumes that cover more specific problems in greater detail than this text (e.g., Guo & Fraser, 2015; Leite, 2017; Pan & Bai, 2015a), this book provides an introduction to the general use and practical applications of PS methods so that after reading this book, the reader should be able to meet the following goals:

1. Understand when it is or is not appropriate to use PS methods, given a researcher's goal, design, and available data;
2. Be able to assess the common support of the estimated propensity scores (i.e., how well the propensity scores are similar across groups);
3. Be able to model and estimate propensity scores that will sufficiently account for selection bias in an observational study;
4. Be familiar with the most common PS methods (i.e., PS matching, subclassification, inverse probability weighting, covariate adjustment, and doubly robust adjustments) and have a sense of how to select the most appropriate method based on their research designs, data, and propensity scores;
5. Know how to use those PS methods;
6. Know how to assess individual covariates for balance across groups;
7. Know how to estimate their adjusted treatment effect;
8. Understand the limitations when using PS methods; and
9. Get to know a variety of software packages used to implement PS methods through the book's website.

The book is structured in this order so that the reader can follow all the steps necessary to complete a PS procedure. Each chapter is devoted to one or two of these goals as listed above. Chapter 1 introduces the basic concepts of making causal inferences from experimental and observational studies, and then discusses propensity scores in terms of *what* they are, *when* to use them, *why* we use them (Goal 1), and the assumptions that need to be met when using them (Goal 2). Chapter 2 focuses on how to select appropriate covariates and model propensity scores (Goal 3). Chapter 3 discusses four commonly used PS methods (matching, stratification, weighting, and covariate adjustment) (Goals 4 and 5). Chapter 4 covers how to evaluate the balance of covariate distributions, how to estimate the adjusted treatment effect, and how robust the treatment effect estimation is against hidden bias (Goals 6 and 7). Chapter 5 summarizes the key points of PS methods, provides some general guidelines for handling common problems with PS methods, and introduces some new developments in PS methods (Goal 8). Finally, the companion website for this book at **study.sagepub .com/researchmethods/qass/bai&clark** provides instructions, code, and interpretations of output for a variety of statistical software packages that are commonly used to implement PS methods (Goal 9).

To help readers better understand the procedures for implementing PS methods, Chapters 2, 3, and 4 include an example of how to apply these procedures to real world data. These examples demonstrate each step of the PS procedures that correspond to what we previously discussed in the chapter. The data are a subset of a dataset that is publicly available from the Inter-University Consortium for Political and Social Research (ICPSR 35683). The data were originally used to assess the Playworks intervention, which is a recess program for elementary school children intended to improve social and emotional skills by teaching safe, engaging forms of play (www.playworks.org). Because software packages often change, the dataset, program codes, outputs, and interpretations of the output are provided on the book's website. Readers are encouraged to replicate the examples using our code and check their results with those we provide online.

1.1 Causal Inference

1.1a Experimental Design and Observational Studies

In an experimental design, it is assumed that we obtain treatment and control groups with equal distributions of group member characteristics (except for the treatment condition) through random sampling and random assignment, thereby limiting potential selection bias, so that the factor of interest is the only cause of an effect. In contrast, researchers conducting an observational study, from which conclusions are drawn based on results from data collected without random assignment, are less confident when making causal inferences. To better understand why this is an issue, in this section we briefly discuss the basic concept of causal inference and illustrate the importance of good research designs.

Suppose that we are interested in studying whether a recess program impacts social skills among elementary school children. According to the counterfactual framework for modeling causal effects, the true treatment effect for each child would be the difference between the treated outcome and the counterfactual (i.e., the outcome in the absence of the treatment) (Holland, 1986; Rubin, 1974). In this context, we would need to compare the social skills of each child who participated in the recess program (the "treatment" participants) to *the same child's* social skills if he or she had not been in the recess program (the counterfactual).

Obviously, we cannot observe social skills under both of these conditions at the same time, since children cannot simultaneously be in the program and not be in the program. Therefore, as a reasonable alternative, one can estimate the *average treatment effect* (ATE) (Holland, 1986; Rubin, 1974; Winship & Morgan, 1999) for the population. To assess the ATE for the children's social skills, we examine the difference between the expected value of social skills for all the children in the recess program and the expected value of social skills for all the children who were not in the recess program. If we randomly select students from the population and randomly assign them into the recess program, the ATE is an unbiased estimate of the treatment effect because the recess (treatment) group does not, on average, differ systematically from those who were not in the recess program (comparison group) on their observed and unobserved background characteristics.

However, in many research situations, randomized control trials (RCTs) or true experiments, in which participants are randomly selected and assigned to groups, are not always feasible. In some research situations, it is not possible to randomly assign participants to conditions, and in others it is not ethical to randomly assign them. For example, it is highly unlikely that we have the ability to manipulate parents' expectations, force people to seek therapy, or control who attends college. Even when random assignment is possible, it may not be ethical to randomly assign participants to risky conditions, such as smoking, alcohol use, cancer, sexually transmitted diseases, child abuse, or homelessness. However, the absence of random assignment should not prevent us from studying how psychotherapy affects depression (Bernstein et al., 2016); how alcohol use affects coronary heart disease (e.g., Fillmore, Kerr, Stockwell, Chikritzhs, & Bostrom, 2006); how maternal smoking influences birth weight and preterm birth (e.g., Ko et al., 2014); or how types of child abuse (physical, sexual, or emotional) impact depression and aggression in its victims (e.g., Vachon, Krueger, Rogosch, & Cicchetti, 2015).

For example, when studying how parents' expectations of their children's academic success influence mathematics achievement, we cannot assign students to parents with high or low expectations, nor can we manipulate parents' expectations. Therefore, it is very likely that students' background characteristics in the two groups are significantly different, which may also influence their math achievement scores. Knowing that students are different on their characteristics other than just their parents' expectations, we cannot directly assess the impact of parents' expectations on students' math achievement using the observational data without controlling for other influential factors. The unbalanced distributions of the influential factors (often called confounding variables or covariates) between the two groups create selection bias, which usually causes a biased ATE. Naturally, our next question is, how can we draw *valid*, causal conclusions from observational studies? The next section addresses how this can be achieved.

1.1b Internal Validity of Observational Studies

A statistical causal inference is a claim made about a cause-and-effect relationship between two or more variables from a statistical model. Therefore, the validity of a statistical causal inference, also called internal validity (Shadish et al., 2002), refers to a researcher making a *reasonable* inference from a statistical analysis of the data in which there is little doubt that a causal relationship exists. Selection bias is a considerable threat to the validity of statistical causal inference in observational studies. As we discussed in the previous section, selection bias refers to systematic differences in distributions of covariates that result in incomparable groups (e.g., people in the treatment group are older, more motivated, or more educated than those in the comparison group). Selection bias typically occurs when observed (measured) covariates or hidden (unmeasured) covariates are not accounted for in statistical models or controlled for in the design, which results in spurious estimates of causal effects (Rosenbaum, 2010). For instance, using the previous example of parents' expectations on students' academic performance, existing literature indicates that students' gender is related to both students' math achievement (Fennema & Sherman, 1997) and parents' expectations. Therefore, gender may be a confounding variable that influences students' math achievement because students cannot be randomly assigned to parents with high expectations or low expectations. In this case, we cannot make any *valid* causal claims regarding the impact of parents' expectations on students' math achievement without controlling for the influence from the confounding factors. Moreover, students' achievement in mathematics is also related to students' personal beliefs (Gutman, 2006; Schommer-Aitkins, Duell, & Hutter, 2005); their peers' influence (Hanushek, Kain, Markman, & Rivkin, 2003); their reading abilities (Hill, Rowan, & Ball, 2005); environmental variables (Koth, Bradshaw, & Leaf, 2008); sociodemographic variables (e.g., ethnicity, socioeconomic status); and school compositions (Entwisle & Alexander, 1992), which may also confound the effect of parents' expectations on student achievement. With many such confounding variables, it is highly unlikely that all of the covariates in the study would be balanced between the high and low expectation groups. If the distributions of these covariates are not balanced, any estimates made without accounting for this imbalance would weaken the validity of the statistical causal inference of the study.

From the above example, it is clear that we cannot directly analyze observational data for causal effect without adjusting or controlling for the confounding variables. The confounding variables can be hidden (not measured), nonmeasurable, or observable (measured and available to the researcher). If these variables are *observable*, it is possible to reduce selection bias and improve the validity of the statistical causal inference by adjusting or controlling for those covariates.

1.1c Existing Methods to Reduce Selection Bias

In many cases, we are not able to randomly select and assign participants to grouping conditions due to the constraints of the specific independent variable (e.g., researchers cannot randomly assign biological sex) or the will of the participants (e.g., participants are more likely to choose or be required to enter a drug rehabilitation program than to be randomly assigned into it). Therefore, we must find some way of balancing nonequivalent groups to increase the validity of causal inference when randomized trials are not feasible. Several approaches that are commonly used to control the influence of covariates and confounding factors are to (a) use designs that test or rule out alternative causal explanations, (b) use designs that balance groups on specific covariates, (c) account for known sources of bias (observed covariates) through statistical models that adjust the treatment effects, and (d) combine two or more of these approaches (Shadish et al., 2002).

The first option is achieved by adding design elements, which are variables or conditions added to a research design to assess threats to validity by varying experimental conditions. These commonly include comparison groups (e.g., control, placebo, partial treatment) or observations over time (e.g., pretests, follow-up measures). For example, adding a sugar pill as a placebo to a medical experiment may help researchers determine whether observed effects are due to the active ingredients in a medication or a patient's belief that the treatment will be effective. Adding a pretest (even when participants are randomly assigned to groups) is common in educational studies, as it allows researchers to examine the difference in learning outcomes after instruction between two or more teaching methods or programs while controlling for preexisting characteristics that may influence students' performance.

While researchers agree that adding relevant elements to quasi-experimental designs can be effective in reducing threats to internal validity (Larzelere & Cox, 2013; Murname & Willett, 2011; Shadish et al., 2002), this approach often requires a considerable amount of advance planning, complex statistical analyses, and available participants. Furthermore, these designs may not be feasible to carry out as a randomized study if assignment to conditions could not be controlled by the researcher.

An instrumental variable (IV) model is another control method that uses a variable that is correlated with the predictor (or causal variable) but is not associated with the change in the outcome variable. An IV can be correlated with the outcome variable, but it must not explain the change in the outcome variable. For example, when attempting to estimate the causal effect of parents' expectations on student achievement in mathematics, the correlation between parents' expectations and students' math scores does not imply that parents' expectations can cause students' math scores to change. Other variables may affect both parents' expectations and student achievement, or student achievement may affect parents' expectations. Since we cannot manipulate parents' expectations of their children, we may estimate the causal effect of parents' expectations on student achievement by using parents' income as an instrument. This assumes that parents' income impacts their expectations, but income is only correlated with student achievement through the effect of parents' expectations. If we find that parents' income and student achievement are correlated, this may be evidence that parents' expectations have a causal effect on student achievement. Unfortunately, despite Bowden and Turkington's (1990) claim that IV models produce results comparable to an experimental design, in practice, it can be difficult to correctly identify appropriate IVs to produce consistent treatment effect estimates (Land & Felson, 1978).

Researchers can also match participants on one or several potentially confounding variables either before or after an intervention to achieve similarity between treatment and control groups (Rubin, 2006). This is usually used in quasi-experimental designs. Although either continuous (e.g., age or parents' income) or categorical (e.g., gender or ethnicity) variables may be used in this matching process, it is easier to match on a couple of categorical variables than on several variables. Despite the common use of this method in quasi-experimental design, traditional matching presents two problems: (a) It is difficult to find exact matches for continuous variables, and (b) it is difficult to match group members on multiple covariates, even with categorical variables. Using the parents' expectation study as an example, if we wanted to match on parents' income, this would require that we find the same parental income (e.g., $65,000) for a child in the treatment group and in the control group. Given the variability of incomes, it is unlikely that we would find many parents in each group that have the same income. Matching on a single categorical variable, such as gender, would not be difficult; however, finding a child in the control group with the same gender, ethnicity, native language, and family composition as each child in the treatment group would limit the number of potential matches. By limiting the number of matches made between the treatment and control groups, the sample size is reduced, which also decreases statistical power and generalizability of research results.

The first problem can be resolved by using proximal matching, which matches members based on *similar* values (e.g., a student whose parents' income is $65,000 can be matched with a student whose parents' income is $64,800), rather than exact values. The second problem *could* be reduced by limiting the number of matching variables to one or two. However, this would also restrict the number of confounding variables that are balanced; therefore, estimated treatment effects are still biased even after matching.

Another common strategy is to control the confounding factors in non-randomized studies by using traditional covariate adjustment, such as analysis of covariance (ANCOVA) or a form of regression (e.g., ordinary least squares or logistic). These approaches partial out the effects of confounding variables on the treatment effect by including covariates in the statistical model (Eisenberg, Downs, & Golberstein, 2012; Jamelske, 2009; Ngai, Chan, & Ip, 2009). In the simplest case, researchers may use a pretest observation as a covariate with the hope of controlling for the group differences on pretest scores. More commonly, researchers will include several other confounding variables as covariates, knowing that treatment groups are probably different on those variables that also influence outcome estimations other than just pretest scores. Even though traditional covariate analyses *can* control for confounding factors to some extent (Leow, Wen, & Korfmacher, 2015; Stürmer et al., 2006), using these approaches presents some theoretical and practical problems. First, these statistical models may be easily misspecified due to small or unequal sample sizes, violations of statistical assumptions, or covariates that may not be able to sufficiently account for confounding due to the limited number of covariates that can be included in a specific model or an unmeasured confounding variable. While adding additional covariates may reduce confounding, each new covariate added to the model will reduce the statistical power.

A second major problem in using traditional covariate adjustments is that these analyses do not directly model bias. That is, covariates are not weighted according to how well they balance covariates, but rather how well they relate to the dependent variable. Therefore, rather than accounting for differences between groups in the covariate, they focus on accounting for the shared variance between the covariate (for all participants) and the outcome variable. For example, in a job training program, if the correlation between the starting and posttest salaries was high (e.g., $r = .7$), the covariate alone would explain 49% of the variance of the posttest salary. While this would still leave 51% of the variance unexplained, the unique contribution of the job training program may not be strong enough to be detected as a significant effect through an ANCOVA model. Despite the popularity of using traditional covariate adjustments to account for selection bias, they may not be appropriate statistical procedures for reducing selection bias.

Another significant limitation of covariance analysis is that including several covariates in the model simultaneously may reduce statistical power. However, if researchers limit the number of covariates, they may fail to control for all influential factors and still end up with a biased estimate of the causal effect. For example, in our job training example, there are many factors related to salary increases, so if we account for only some of these factors, the effect of job training on salary increase may not be estimated correctly. Therefore, only in some cases will covariance analysis be effective in controlling for the confounding factors from selection bias. Thus, it is clear that we need better methods. Although there are a variety of procedures that suitably model and reduce selection bias in observational studies (e.g., Camillo & D'Attoma, 2010; Heckman, 1979), some of the most widely used approaches use propensity scores (Rosenbaum & Rubin, 1983). The following sections will focus on the basic concepts related to this approach.

1.2 Propensity Scores

1.2a What Is a Propensity Score?

A propensity score is the probability that a participant would be assigned to a particular study group based on a set of covariates (Rosenbaum & Rubin, 1983). Most often, propensity scores are estimated as the likelihood that a person would be assigned or self-select into a treatment condition (see Chapter 2 for details as to how they are computed). As probabilities, propensity scores range from 0 to 1. Scores above .5 predict that a participant will be in the treatment group, and those below .5 predict that a participant will be in the control or comparison group. However, the goal of propensity scores is not to perfectly predict assignment condition, but to create a single composite score to represent the whole set of covariates that can be used to account for group differences on all observed characteristics or confounding factors due to selection. This also assumes that participants with the same propensity scores will have the same distributions of observed covariates between the treatment and comparison groups. As such, the propensity score can then be used with a variety of statistical adjustments that should make the background characteristics or covariates of the participants in the treatment group comparable to those in the control or comparison group—as one would see with random assignment (Rosenbaum & Rubin, 1983). Common statistical adjustments used in PS methods include (a) matching, which pairs participants from treatment and control groups based on the proximity of their propensity scores; (b) sub-classification (or stratification), which groups participants who are matched on several strata based on their propensity scores; (c) weighting, which multiplies outcome observations by a weight based on the propensity score; and (d) covariate adjustment, which uses propensity scores as a covariate in an ANCOVA or regression. These adjustment methods and how to conduct them are described more fully in Chapter 3. In theory, PS methods should balance the treatment groups on all of the observed covariates used to compute the propensity scores and reduce the bias caused by nonrandom assignment. If propensity scores are modeled appropriately, the adjusted treatment effects should be unbiased (Rosenbaum & Rubin, 1985).

1.2b Why Use Propensity Scores?

PS methods may not be our first choice in controlling for bias in research, but they may be the best alternative to random assignment, as they address selection bias at the design level, as opposed to other statistical control procedures. As discussed in Section 1.1c, several existing methods can be used to control for confounding variables in observational studies. Under certain conditions, these methods can be effective in reducing bias. However, they also have several limitations, many of which PS methods can reduce. Like instrumental variables, covariate matching, and covariate adjustments, PS methods can also be conducted on existing data. Therefore, they permit the use of archival data to balance nonequivalent groups when designs cannot be altered.

While both the instrumental variable approach and covariate matching can reduce bias, these procedures only allow researchers to balance groups on the variables included in these adjustments. In many cases, only a single variable is used as the instrumental variable, which needs to meet certain conditions that can be difficult to operate or identify (e.g., it must correlate with the treatment variable, but not the change in the outcome variable). Since it is probable that selection bias is affected by several variables, not all of these would be equally distributed between the treatment and control groups. Therefore, even if the instrumental variable meets the conditions for a certain analysis, selection bias may not be sufficiently reduced.

When matching on multiple covariates, it is very difficult to match on all of them simultaneously, as each additional covariate limits the number of viable matches. This often means that researchers must either match on several variables with limited levels (e.g., biological sex with options for only male or female, or age with options for only young or old) or select only a few influential variables with several levels (e.g., high school GPA or ACT when participants self-select into college). A better solution would be to use a composite score that aggregates several variables into one.

As a composite score, a propensity score combines the simplicity and statistical power of using a single score with the thoroughness of using multiple covariates by accounting for the variance of several variables concurrently (Rosenbaum & Rubin, 1983). Propensity scores aggregate multiple covariates into a single score, and covariates are weighted in a way that considers their relative importance in assignment to conditions. This solves the problems presented not just when using instrumental variables and covariate matching, but when using traditional covariate adjustment too.

Although traditional covariate adjustment can accommodate several covariates, statistical power can still be affected when trying to include several covariates, especially when using a small sample size. More importantly, propensity scores actually model selection bias, not the predictability of the dependent variable. Therefore, by using PS methods, researchers can actually account for statistical estimation *bias* from model misspecification due to design issues, rather than how the individual covariates relate to the outcome variable. This is why matching, stratifying, or statistical adjustments using propensity scores often reduce selection bias better than analysis of covariance or multivariate models (Grunwald & Mayhew, 2008; Peterson et al., 2003).

Despite the advantages that PS methods have over other methods used to reduce selection bias, propensity scores still have their limitations. Several conditions and assumptions should be met when using propensity scores, which are discussed in the next few sections. Like most statistics, if these assumptions are not met, propensity scores may not effectively reduce selection bias. These limitations and ways of addressing them are discussed in greater detail in Chapter 5.

1.2c When to Use Propensity Scores

PS methods have been used to reduce group selection bias or adjust treatment effects in nonrandomized experiments in a variety of behavioral and social science fields (Baycan, 2016; Gunter & Daly, 2012; Kirchmann et al., 2012), and their use has increased exponentially within the past few decades (Bai, 2011). Unfortunately, their increased popularity could also lead to misuse (Pan & Bai, 2016). Like most statistical methods, they are appropriate only under certain conditions. PS methods are intended to balance group data when treatment assignment is nonignorable (e.g., assignment is not random, clearly specified, or maintained by participants); assess treatment effects when using quasi-experiments or other types of group comparisons using observational data; and aggregate several covariates into a single variable (the propensity score) to be used for statistical adjustments (Guo & Fraser, 2015; Shadish, 2010).

Because PS methods were created to improve internal validity, they should be used when researchers attempt to draw causal inferences from their observational studies. Propensity scores are used to account for preexisting individual characteristics that may be related to the treatment conditions tested for causal effects; therefore, we must be able to establish that the intended cause (even if it isn't a treatment or intervention) precedes the effect.

While propensity scores can be applied to a variety of nonrandomized experiments, they are intended to test causal effects from observational studies in which the assignment method is unknown. This may include quasi-experiments, natural experiments, or causal comparative studies. Within these studies, there are several ways in which assignment can be nonrandom, but corrected with PS methods:

1. Participants may have self-selected into a treatment. For example, when examining how the mode of instruction affects academic performance in college students, students may choose to sign up for an online course (treatment) instead of a face-to-face course (comparison) because it fits their schedules.

2. Someone assigned participants to groups based on an inconsistent or unknown criterion. If more than one person is determining who gets into the treatment, each person may use different standards for admission, or administrators may make exceptions for some by altering the criterion. For example, some children may be admitted to a gifted education program simply because they have ability scores that exceed 130, while others (who demonstrate high motivation to success or independence) are admitted with scores of 120.

3. The causal variable is not directly manipulated by the researcher. In cases of causal comparative or natural experiments, the event or

characteristic that we assume is causal is not a treatment or intervention that is imposed by a researcher; it is an existing characteristic or accidental event. Examples of these may include biological sex, birth order, marital status, socioeconomic status, and medical condition. A more specific example is illustrated in Almond's (2006) study that examined the effects of prenatal exposure to influenza on long-term health, education, and economic outcomes.

In all of these examples, the reasons for participants' assignment to treatment conditions is unknown or unclear, and using PS methods would be appropriate. However, if the assignment is based on a known (and maintained) criterion, such as when alcoholics are assigned to substance abuse programs based on the severity of their addictions, a regression discontinuity design (RDD) may be more effective and easier to use than PS methods. In theory, an RDD works under the same principles as a randomized control trial, in that we know the selection mechanism; therefore, we can control for it. By assigning participants to groups based on the value of a baseline characteristic, this serves as a proxy to random assignment and should account for selection bias. According to Shadish (2010), "Such assignment is called ignorable because potential outcomes are unrelated to treatment assignment once those known variables are included in the model, so an unbiased estimate can still be obtained" (p. 6). However, this assumes that the criterion for assignment is strictly followed, and that if participants are assigned to groups based on more than one variable, all assignment variables are included in the statistical model.

Finally, to balance covariates on several characteristics, researchers must have several measured covariates, which are related to both selection into conditions and the outcome variable, available to include in PS models. If researchers conduct their study using secondary data that is limited to a few demographic covariates, it is unlikely that they will be able to sufficiently model the selection process. In such cases, propensity score methods may not sufficiently reduce bias (Steiner, Cook, Shadish, & Clark, 2010). Therefore, it is recommended that researchers consider what variables are likely to influence assignment to conditions *before* data are collected so that these can be measured or use existing data with sufficient covariates.

1.3 Assumptions

1.3a The Ignorable Treatment Assignment Assumption

One of the assumptions when using PS methods is that assignment to treatment conditions is independent of the treatment effect after accounting for a set of observed covariates. In a randomized experiment, this assumption is often met even without accounting for covariates, since (on expectation) random assignment balances all covariates between treatment conditions. Of course, this assumption is not guaranteed in a quasi-experiment, particularly when participants self-select into conditions. Under this assumption, if the distributions of the propensity scores are balanced between the treatment conditions, the distributions of the covariates used for obtaining propensity scores are also equal between the treatment conditions. Therefore, we assume that selection bias has been eliminated (or sufficiently reduced) after making statistical adjustments with the propensity scores, provided that all the confounding variables are measured. This is why we use PS methods in the first place.

One way to verify that selection bias has been reduced after using PS adjustments is to examine the relationship between treatment conditions and each observed covariate. A difference between the group means (or proportions when covariates are categorical) suggests that the covariate is unbalanced and violates this assumption. Chapter 4 more fully describes various methods for testing the balance of covariates.

Of course, we can only test for covariate balance on the variables that we measured and included in the PS estimation model. Although researchers should attempt to control for all reasonable sources of bias in the set of observed covariates used to estimate the propensity scores, it is likely that some unmeasured or unobserved covariates are not included; thus, selection bias remains even after PS adjustments. In this case, these omitted variables are sources of hidden bias that still affect treatment effects.

For example, if a covariate, such as risk for child abuse, is related to treatment assignment and the outcome, but is not included in the PS estimation, the treatment effects will still be biased. When the propensity scores calculated from the set of covariates do not represent all influential covariates, they cannot balance the distributions of all covariates between the groups. In this case, the ignorable treatment assignment assumption is not met using PS methods. When covariates were limited to only a few commonly available demographic covariates (e.g., age, ethnicity, sex, and marital status), less than half of the selection bias was removed (Steiner et al., 2010). Therefore, it is essential that all the covariates that contribute to selection bias are included in the PS model. Chapter 2 provides more guidance on how to select covariates so that this assumption is met.

1.3b The Stable Unit Treatment Value Assumption

The second assumption when using PS methods is that the treatment effect for each individual will not depend on how each person gets into his or her respective condition. This requires that (a) the outcome does not depend on the assignment procedure (i.e., randomized or self-selection) and

(b) the treatment is the same for all participants in the treatment group (Holmes, 2014; Rosenbaum & Rubin, 1983). According to Cox (1958), "The observation of one unit should be unaffected by the particular assignment of treatment to the other units" (p. 19). When implementing PS methods, such as PS matching, the stable unit treatment value assumption (SUTVA) assumes that (a) within a matched pair, Participant A in the treatment group and Participant B in the control group have the same likelihood of being assigned to the treatment or control group; and (b) Participant A receives the same type and amount of treatment as the other participants in the treatment group who were selected through PS matching.

SUTVA is violated when the outcome depends on the version of the treatment participants receive or when there is an interaction between participants that would allow them to share the treatment. This can also be explained in terms of specific threats to validity: (a) unreliability of treatment implementation, in which treatment is not given consistently to each person in the treatment condition; (b) compensatory equalization, when participants in the control group receive an alternate version of the treatment; (c) compensatory rivalry, when participants in the control group are motivated to perform as well on the outcome as those in the treatment group; (d) resentful demoralization, when participants in the control group reduce their effort on the outcome because they did not receive the treatment; and (e) treatment diffusion, when the participants in the control group learn the treatment for those in the treatment group (Shadish et al., 2002). Under these circumstances, the participants did not receive the treatment (or lack of treatment) that they were assigned to receive. Clearly, we cannot make reasonable inferences about the effect of treatment if a participant actually receives a different treatment.

1.3c Sufficient Common Support or Overlap

The third assumption implies that there is sufficient overlap in the distributions of the propensity scores estimated for the treatment and control groups; that is, the two groups being compared share a common support region of propensity scores in the sample data. This presumes that participants with the same propensity scores have an equal chance of being in either the treatment or control group based on the similarity of their background characteristics or covariates, which would allow us to isolate the treatment and make a reasonable (unbiased) comparison between the two groups. For example, if two employees both have a propensity score of .7, each has a 70% chance of being in a job training program based on his or her background characteristics. Then, we can reasonably compare their salaries after one completes the training program while the other does not.

If most of the members in the treatment group have propensity scores that are similar to those in the control group, we assume that the two groups are comparable. The proportion of the similarity of the propensity scores of the treatment and control or comparison groups is called common support. If the comparison groups do not have sufficient common support, they are not comparable; therefore, PS methods should not be used.

Even though propensity scores are the predicted probabilities of selection into a condition, the goal of PS methods is not to predict group membership, but to use propensity scores to balance treatment and control groups. The best cases for PS methods are actually those who are assigned to the treatment group, but are just as likely to be in the control group (and vice versa). Ideally, the PS distributions for both the treatment and control groups would be normal and have a mean of .5 with equal standard deviations. Under these conditions, we are most likely to replicate random assignment, as participants in one group will be very similar to those in the other group, which will allow one to obtain an unbiased treatment effect. However, we may not always see these distributions, especially when using several covariates that are strongly related to selection. Sometimes, we find that those in the treatment group have higher propensity scores than those in the control group. Therefore, in some situations, we may need to improve the common support by having more variability in the propensity scores of those in the control group compared with those in the treatment group, which may be achieved by having proportionally more participants in the control group who can be matched to those in the treatment group.

There are several methods for examining common support, such as the following: (a) making a visual inspection of the PS distributions, (b) comparing the minimum and maximum values of the propensity scores of each group, (c) using a trimming procedure (d) running an inferential test to determine if the distributions are *significantly* different from each other, or (e) estimating the mean difference of the propensity scores.

For the first method, researchers may simply graph PS distributions for the treatment and control groups and visually inspect the extent to which they overlap (Bai, 2013; Shadish, Clark, & Steiner, 2008). This can be done by comparing histograms or boxplots of the distributions of propensity scores for each group. As shown in Figure 1.1, nearly all of the propensity scores for those in the treatment group are between .03 and .5, while the propensity scores for the control group are between 0 and .8. Therefore, the area of common support (indicated by the box over the distributions) is between .03 and .5; those with propensity scores above .5 and below .03 do not have comparable matches.

Figure 1.1 The propensity score distributions for the treatment and control groups

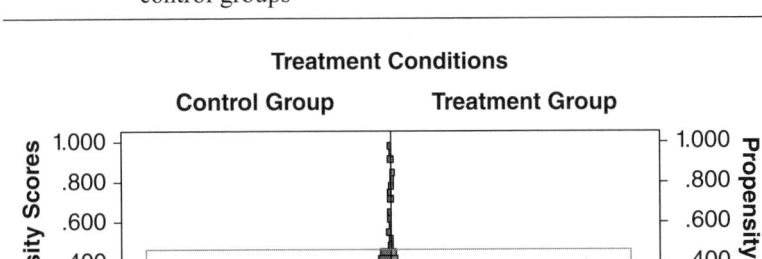

For the second method, one would "delete all observations whose propensity score is smaller than the minimum and larger than the maximum in the opposite group" (Caliendo & Kopeinig, 2008, p. 45). For example, if propensity scores in the treatment group range from .03 to .9 and the propensity scores in the control group range from 0 to .8, the overlapping distribution (or common support) is between .03 and .8.

The third method was used by Smith and Todd (2005), by which they identified the range of propensity scores that had a positive density within both distributions. This method not only excludes the observations in which the propensity scores do not overlap, but also drops cases with low frequencies of propensity scores in each group. For example, suppose that all overlapping propensity scores are between .03 and .8, but there are very few cases in one group or both groups with propensity scores between .5 and .8. In this approach, not only would we exclude all cases with propensity scores that were greater than .8 or less than .03, but we would also drop participants in the control group whose propensity scores were greater than .5. Likewise, if there were very few cases in the treatment group with propensity scores between .03 and .1, these cases would also be dropped (Caliendo & Kopeinig, 2008).

The fourth method consists of using an inferential statistic, such as the independent samples Kolmogorov-Smirnov test, to determine whether or not there is a significant difference between the distributions of the propensity scores for the treatment and control groups (Diamond & Sekhon, 2013). A significant difference between the two distributions would indicate poor common support. However, this method is not recommended for the same reason that *covariate* balance should not be assessed with inferential tests: because "balance is a characteristic of the observed sample, not some hypothetical population" (Ho, Imai, King, & Stuart, 2007, p. 221). In the fifth method, researchers compute the standardized difference score ($d = (M_T - M_C)/s_p$) to compare the means of the propensity scores for the treatment (M_T) and control groups (M_C). A small difference score (i.e., $d < .5$) indicates good common support.

Unfortunately, what constitutes *sufficient* common support is still not clear, since not all of these methods provide a clear criterion. The visual inspection using graphs and the minima and maxima comparison may provide clear criteria for cases that share common characteristics, but we do not know how much of this shared support is sufficient. While researchers have offered some guidelines, their standards are not universally recognized. For example, Bai (2015) found that selection bias is most likely to be reduced with PS matching if at least 75% of the propensity scores overlap in each distribution. If using the method of comparing the standard mean differences, Rubin (2001) recommends that the standardized mean difference between the group distributions is less than .5.

However, these general guidelines may not be sufficient when considering that the specific method of determining common support and (more importantly) of how to handle common support depends on the distributions of the data and the particular matching methods used to adjust the treatment effects. For example, if distributions are skewed or have many outliers, the inferential test or trimming procedure may assess common support better than the minima and maxima comparison or the standardized mean difference. Also, the specific method of matching will address how the degree of common support is managed. Caliper matching (see Chapter 3) uses cases with the best common support (or closest PS matches), while stratification is more lenient in its requirements for common support by allowing more flexibility in the acceptable matches. It is important to understand that how common support (or more importantly, how a lack of common support) is handled influences the validity of the results of the estimated treatment effect when using PS methods. Regardless of how common support is assessed, the defined region of common support determines which cases remain in the analyses. For instance, those cases with propensity scores outside of the range of common support may or may not be included in the final outcome analyses, depending on the specific PS method selected. If PS matching with a caliper is used, the cases with propensity scores outside of the range of common support are usually excluded in the final sample selected to estimate the treatment effect. While this restriction of cases improves the ability to match comparable cases and presumably improve internal validity, it also poses potential problems to external and statistical conclusion validity. First, it may limit our ability to generalize the study results to the population. That is, if the cases that we dropped (i.e., those who are very likely to be selected for treatment) were systematically different from those who remained in the analysis (i.e., those who were just as likely to be selected into the treatment group as the control group), the sample selected may no longer represent its original population. Second, dropping cases will reduce the sample size, which may affect statistical power. Excluding only a few cases from a dataset with a large sample size is not problematic, but dropping half the cases from an already small sample may underpower the analysis for the treatment effect. Type II errors are just as misleading as selection bias. Therefore, if the common support is not sufficient, PS methods should not be used.

1.4 Summary of the Chapter

PS methods can be effective in reducing selection bias in observational data and increasing the validity of statistical causal inference when used appropriately. More specifically, they can (a) control for multiple covariates using one composite score, (b) balance the influences from covariates on causal effect estimation when used as weights or covariate adjustments, and (c) create balanced groups that mimic those in true experimental designs. Under many conditions, PS methods are preferable to other methods used to reduce selection bias. However, it is important to note that, for propensity scores to be most effective, the conditions and assumptions that were discussed previously in this chapter must be met. The checklist below is provided to help you determine whether or not a PS method is suitable for your observational study. Assuming that it is, the next steps are to learn how to estimate and apply propensity scores. In the following chapters, we will focus on the practical applications of PS methods with an empirical example throughout the book to illustrate how to use PS methods.

Checklist for Using Propensity Score Methods

☑ You plan to examine the causal relationship between a treatment and an outcome.

☑ You are not certain how participants were assigned to treatment groups.

☑ You are familiar with theoretical or empirical evidence for why participants might choose (or be assigned to) treatment groups.

(Continued)

(Continued)

- ☑ You have access to several measured covariates that are related to the treatment condition and the outcome variable(s).
- ☑ The set of available covariates will include nearly all confounding factors that impact causal variables and outcomes.
- ☑ There is sufficient overlap in the PS distributions between the treatment and control groups.
- ☑ There is very little missing data within each covariate.
- ☑ Measures of the covariates are valid and reliable.

Study Questions for Chapter 1

1. What is a group selection bias?
2. What is a propensity score?
3. When should researchers use PS methods instead of other methods to control for selection bias?
4. How do PS methods control for selection bias?
5. When might PS methods not sufficiently reduce bias?

CHAPTER 2. COVARIATE SELECTION AND PROPENSITY SCORE ESTIMATION

In the previous chapter, we focused on the conditions and assumptions under which it is appropriate to use PS methods. Once we have determined that our research and data would benefit from propensity scores, our next step is to create the propensity scores. For this, we must select the covariates, determine an appropriate statistical model, and use a statistical procedure to estimate the propensity scores. Because the aim of the PS methods is to balance the distributions of the covariates between the treatment and comparison groups, we need to keep this goal in mind as we model the propensity scores. Since the effectiveness of PS methods depends on having good covariates, this chapter will discuss how to select appropriate covariates and model their relationships with group selection in a way that will effectively reduce selection bias. At the end of this chapter, we will demonstrate how to select covariates for a model that will estimate propensity scores using the Playworks data. A more detailed description of the data is provided in Section 2.4a, and the data, code, and output for several statistical software packages (e.g., R and SPSS) are provided on the course website. By the end of this chapter, you should be able to model and estimate propensity scores that will sufficiently account for selection bias in an observational study.

2.1 Covariate Selection

2.1a Covariate Selection Mechanisms

Covariate selection mechanisms are the criteria used when selecting covariates for a PS model. While not all researchers follow the same criteria, most generally agree that covariate selection should be guided by two major considerations: (a) the theoretical framework for why and how particular variables are related to treatment conditions and outcomes, and (b) how well the potential covariates are statistically related to the treatment conditions and outcome variables.

Relationships of the covariates with the treatment conditions and outcome variables. Ideally, based on the counterfactual theory (Lewis, 1973), the participants assigned to treatment and control conditions should be identical in all aspects except the treatment conditions to assess a causal effect. However, in empirical studies, it is more practical and necessary to balance the groups only on the confounders and variables that may actually influence the treatment effect. Therefore, when considering covariates for the PS model, we need to start by assessing the relationships of each covariate with the treatment conditions and outcome variables. The best covariates for the PS estimation model are those that are related to both the treatment condition and the outcome variable. Since the primary goal of propensity scores is to model how participants are related to a particular treatment condition, it is important that the covariates can predict selection. If the covariates are also statistically related to the outcome, this indicates that they influence the outcome. Having a relationship with both condition and outcome is what causes bias. Therefore, these variables are considered to be nonignorable and must be in the PS model to sufficiently account for bias (see Chapter 1, Section 1.3 for more on this). However, covariates do not have to be related to *both* treatment condition and the outcome variable to be included in the PS model. Having an influence on only one of them may warrant including that covariate in the PS model.

If a covariate is correlated with the outcome variable, but not with the treatment condition, it will still influence the outcome estimation and needs to be included in the PS model (Brookhart et al., 2006; Rubin & Thomas, 1996). For example, suppose we want to assess the impact that a job training program, which focuses on specific technical skills, has on improving employees' self-competence in completing a job. While we find that employees' technical skills can influence their self-competence, so does the frequency of a supervisor's praise on employees' work. Assuming that the supervisor's praise is not included as a part of the training, the supervisor's praise may confound the estimated treatment effect. That is, those in the comparison group may not receive the same amount of praise from their supervisors as those in the training program. Therefore, the differences in self-competence between the groups will depend not only on their participation in the training program, but also on the amount of praise they receive. Thus, it is essential to balance the frequency of praise between the training and comparison groups to get an unbiased effect on self-competency. In this example, it is necessary to include *praise* as a covariate in the PS estimation model, even though it is not associated with the treatment condition.

When a variable is associated with the treatment condition, but not the outcome variable, the decision to include or exclude that variable from the PS estimation model depends on the nature of the relationship between the potential covariate and the treatment condition (Brookhart et al., 2006). If the covariate *has an impact on the treatment*, it *should* be included in the PS estimation model, as it could still indirectly alter the treatment effect. For example, suppose that a psychologist uses cognitive behavioral therapy (CBT) as a treatment for social anxiety disorder, but is aware that her clients' self-understanding influences their experiences in therapy. While self-understanding is not directly related to social anxiety disorder (e.g., those with a social anxiety disorder may have a weak or strong self-understanding), clients with strong self-understanding are usually more responsive to CBT than those with poor self-understanding. In this case, self-understanding influences the treatment experience; that is, the treatment effect may be different depending on clients' level of self-understanding. Therefore, self-understanding should be included as a covariate when estimating the propensity score. If the covariate is associated with the treatment conditions, but *does not have an impact on the treatment* (nor is it related to the outcome variable), it *should not* be included in the model. Building on the previous example, suppose that CBT is also used to treat eating disorders, but having an eating disorder is not related to having a social anxiety disorder. Cognitive behavioral therapy may reduce symptoms of both eating disorders and social anxiety disorders; however, there is no correlation between the symptoms of the two disorders. In this situation, eating disorders do not influence the CBT treatment or its effect on social anxiety. If the temporal relationship is such that CBT influences eating disorder symptoms, but eating disorder symptoms do not influence CBT, it is not necessary to include eating disorder symptoms as a covariate. In fact, including eating disorder symptoms in the PS model may be detrimental, as it could increase the estimation errors and prevent group balance on the true confounding factors. While it may be beneficial to include variables that are only associated with treatment conditions, this is conditional on whether or not the variable affects the treatment. If the variable does influence the treatment, the variable should be included as a covariate in the PS estimation model; otherwise, it should not.

2.1b Theoretical Foundations for Covariate Selection

The above three situations for selecting covariates cannot be done without having a theoretical foundation or being supported by existing evidence. Therefore, researchers should use theories or previous studies as references to determine which confounding factors or variables are associated with the treatment and the outcome variables. A thorough review of the literature is the first step when selecting the covariates for the PS estimation model. Following conventional practices when selecting covariates, researchers using propensity scores should reference the existing literature to provide theoretical foundations to identify the confounding variables. Just as one might do in a traditional covariate adjustment, we are looking for covariates supported by literature that need to be controlled for in the statistical models so that we may partial out the effect of those variables and obtain a better estimate of the treatment effect. Both traditional covariance analyses and PS methods have the same purpose: to increase the accuracy of the outcome estimation. However, the difference between PS modeling and traditional covariate adjustment is in how the variables are modeled. When selecting covariates for a traditional covariate adjustment (i.e., multiple regression or ANCOVA), researchers may be limited in the number of covariates that they can include, since each additional covariate reduces the available degrees of freedom and the statistical power of an inferential test. Since propensity scores aggregate many covariates into a single score, there is no need to limit the number of covariates that can be included in a PS model. Although we do not advocate including *every* available covariate, do not exclude necessary covariates for fear of having too many. As long as the covariates are appropriate, the more that are included in the PS estimation model, the more likely the groups will be balanced after applying the PS methods (Rosenbaum & Rubin, 1985).

Furthermore, remember that traditional covariate analyses only deal with confounding factors at the analysis level, while PS methods handle these variables at the design level (and sometimes at both the design and analysis levels). The latter provides two benefits over the former. First, modeling the propensity scores based on covariates' relationships with treatment assignment, as opposed to directly controlling for them in statistical models, makes the groups more comparable to randomized experimental designs (Rosenbaum & Rubin, 1985). Second, PS modeling allows researchers to select parsimonious statistical models for treatment estimations after removing the selection bias at the design level. Therefore, when searching for appropriate covariates in existing literature, one needs to consider what factors influence treatment assignment as well as what factors influence the outcome.

2.1c Procedures to Determine Appropriate Covariates

Identifying the covariate pool. It is essential to know how to identify *which* variables will serve as appropriate covariates when reviewing the literature. Existing studies and theories are always the first resource that helps us identify the correct confounding variables as stated in the previous section. For example, when we examine how the type of university (i.e., public or private) impacts graduation rates, we need to control for factors that (a) influence students' choice in universities and (b) relate to the probability that they will complete their degrees. A vast amount of literature indicates that many factors that impact students' graduation rates also influence their college selection. These factors include students' academic readiness, such as SAT, ACT, or equivalent scores (Hernandez, 2000); financial status, such as parents' income, availability of student loans, and eligibility for scholarships (Nora, 2001; Tinto, 1994); and school environments, such as religious affiliation or ethnic diversity (Lane, 2002). Since all of these variables are directly related to both students' selection into the university and whether they graduate on time, they should be considered for inclusion in the PS estimation model.

Consideration of research situations. Researchers typically face two common research situations to answer research questions: (a) to conduct a research study by designing the study and collecting data according to that design, or (b) to use existing or secondary data that are available to us. The mechanism for selecting the covariates is slightly different for each situation. When designing the study from the beginning, researchers should collect data on all possible covariates suggested by the literature. For studies using secondary data, researchers should consider and assess all the available covariates for inclusion in the PS model. While we can only include variables that are available, it is still important to recognize variables that are not available but may still have some impact on the selection bias (i.e., the literature suggests that parents' income affects selection bias, but researchers do not have information on parents' income). Not including these variables violates the assumption of ignorable treatment assignment (see Section 1.3a) and is a limitation to the results that we find when estimating the treatment effects. After obtaining data on the covariates in both research situations, the following steps should be followed to determine the final covariates to be included in the PS estimation model.

Preliminary statistical assessment. We assume that after reviewing the relevant literature, we will have identified all the covariates that need to be included in the PS model and those that should be excluded (e.g., those with neither an impact on treatment conditions nor a relationship to the outcome). In practice, we first need to examine the correlations between the covariates and the outcome variables and treatment conditions. If the correlation is statistically significant for both outcome and treatment conditions, it should be considered for the pool of covariates that is used to estimate the PS model (Brookhart et al., 2006). Second, we need to carefully examine those variables that are only significantly related to outcome variables. If the correlation is significant, we need to include the variable in the PS estimation model. Third, if the variables alter the treatment conditions, they should be included in the PS estimation model.

2.1d Collinearity and Overcorrection

Often overlooked issues concerning covariate selection are collinearity among the covariates and overcorrecting covariates that were well-balanced before applying PS methods. First, covariate multicollinearity in PS models is problematic in a way similar to that found in inferential statistical testing. If the covariates in a PS model are highly correlated, only the covariates that provide unique contributions to the PS estimation model need to be included to balance the group distributions on all of the highly correlated covariates. In the school selection example, students' family income and the number of hours they work are strongly related. Therefore, including only one of the two variables in the PS model will provide the same covariate balance between groups as including both variables. That is, if we are able to balance the groups on family income by including only that variable in the model, we will concurrently balance the number of hours students work too, even though that variable was not included in the PS model.

Another potential problem is overcorrection, which occurs when a specific covariate becomes less balanced between the groups after implementation of the PS method than it was prior to using the method. In many observational studies, some variables are already balanced or less biased without any adjustments. However, when propensity scores are estimated from all of the available covariates, those covariates that are already balanced may be adjusted along with the other covariates in the model. In this case, the individual covariates that were already balanced might now be biased (Bai, 2013; Hirano & Imbens, 2001; Stone & Tang, 2013). Therefore, when selecting covariates to include in the PS model, we need to consider how the covariates work together as well as their individual relationships with the treatment conditions and outcome.

2.2 Propensity Score Estimation

When Rosenbaum and Rubin (1983) first introduced propensity scores, they recommended using "an appropriate logit model (Cox, 1970) or discriminant score" (p. 47) to estimate propensity scores because the true propensity score is usually unknown. In practice, propensity scores can be estimated using logistic regression, discriminate function analysis, classification and regression trees, or neural networks. Of these, logistic regression is the most commonly used approach due to its relative simplicity and effectiveness in balancing the covariates. Tree-based methods, such as classification and regression trees, are also frequently used (Westreich, Lessler, & Funk, 2010), and both methods are often used to create multiple models that are averaged together in procedures called ensemble methods.

2.2a Logistic Regression

Logistic regression is a type of binary logit analysis in which a dichotomous dependent variable is estimated with a regression model. Like an ordinary least squares regression, a logistic regression can accommodate both continuous and categorical predictor variables, making it more versatile than multiway frequency analyses or cluster analyses. While a logistic regression can easily accommodate only categorical predictors using an ordinary least squares or weighted least squares approach, a maximum likelihood approach is necessary when including continuous predictors (Allison, 2012). Using this approach, the estimated coefficients for the predictor variables are those that are most likely to predict the observed outcome values of the dependent variable in the sample (Pampel, 2000).

When using a logistic regression to estimate propensity scores, all of the observed covariates are concurrently included in the model as predictor variables to predict the treatment or assignment condition. The treatment variable must be dichotomous, usually coded as 0 to indicate a comparison or control condition and 1 to indicate the treatment condition. The covariates can be either continuous or categorical. However, if categorical variables have more than two levels, they will need to be recoded into dummy variables. As with an ordinary least squares regression, a regression equation is created from the estimated coefficients for each covariate. The predicted probabilities that are estimated from the regression equation are the propensity scores. Each propensity score can range from 0 to 1 and serves as an estimate of the probability that a participant will be in a particular (usually the treatment) group. Therefore, a propensity score close to 0 indicates that a participant has the characteristics of someone in the control or comparison group, and someone with a propensity score close to 1 has the characteristics of someone in the treatment group. Cases with the same propensity scores share common characteristics.

Drawing on the previous example from Chapter 1, suppose that we are interested in studying whether parents' expectations for their child's academic attainment influence students' mathematics achievement scores. Suppose that we want to include gender, socioeconomic status, and self-confidence in math as covariates. In this case, using a logistic regression, we would create propensity scores that model how our covariates predict parents' expectations.

The regression equation would be

$$u = \beta_0 + \beta_1 X_{1i} + \beta_2 X_{2i} + \beta_3 X_{3i}, \qquad (2.1)$$

where u is the logit model from the logistic regression, which is a linear function of the log of the odds that an outcome will occur depending on the value of a predictor variable. In this example, β_0 is the constant; β_1, β_2, and β_3 are the regression weights that represent the strength of the relationship between each covariate and parents' level of expectation; and X_{1i}, X_{2i}, and X_{3i} would be each student's values on gender, socioeconomic status (SES), and self-confidence in math (confidence), respectively. If the logistic regression produced results for the regression coefficients as $\beta_0 = -0.87$, $\beta_1 = 0.46$, $\beta_2 = 1.19$, and $\beta_3 = 0.29$, the regression equation would be

$$u = -0.87 + 0.46X_{1i} + 1.19X_{2i} + 0.29X_{3i}$$

The propensity scores for individual students would then be based on Equation 2.2:

$$\hat{e}(X_i) = \frac{1}{1+e^{-[-0.87+0.46X_{1i}+1.19X_{2i}+0.29X_{3i}]}} \qquad (2.2)$$

where $e(X_i)$ is the propensity score or predicted probability that a particular student will have a parent with high expectations.

Table 2.1 provides an example of propensity scores for three students based on their covariate values. Because the first student, Alberto, has a high propensity score, it is very likely that his parents have a high academic expectation for him, whereas it is very likely that Cameron's parents have low expectations for him. Since Bianca's propensity score is close to .5, her parents are just as likely to have high expectations as low expectations.

Table 2.1 An Example of Estimated Propensity Scores and the Covariates

Student	Gender	SES	Confidence	Propensity Score
Alberto	0	1	3.7	.8
Bianca	1	0	1.4	.5
Cameron	0	0	0.1	.3

2.2b Tree-Based Methods

Decision tree methods, also known as recursive partitioning, are nonparametric statistics that permit researchers to group participants based on similarities of several covariates. Groups are made based on various ways of splitting data using decision rules that describe the relationships between the predictor variables and dependent variable. Like logistic regression, both continuous and categorical predictor variables can be used, and the resulting values are probabilities that participants will be in one group over another. A classification and regression tree (CART) procedure examines each predictor variable for how well it creates two distinctly different samples "with respect to the dependent variable, according to a predetermined splitting criterion" (Lemon, Roy, Clark, Friedmann, & Rakowski, 2003, p. 173). The predictor variable that can produce the most distinctive split is used first. A second split of the data is made based on the second most influential predictor variable, and subsequent splits are made based on the remaining predictor variables. The result is a tree-like structure with a series of hierarchical branches that represent each split of the sample. To avoid overfitting a model to a particular dataset, classification trees may be "pruned," by which the number of splits is limited. In the context of creating propensity scores, the probability of being in the treatment group is estimated at each split or node. Therefore, the terminal branches represent small groups of participants with a certain probability of assignment, which is the propensity score. Therefore, many participants will likely share the same propensity score, which is less likely to occur when using logistic regression to estimate propensity scores. This may provide an advantage over logistic regression when using certain types of PS methods, such as full matching or stratification, which we will discuss in Chapter 3.

2.2c Ensemble Methods

Ensemble methods use existing PS estimators but create several models of propensity scores that vary based on subsets of the covariates or participants. These models are then averaged together to create a single, stable model. Bootstrap aggregation, also known as bagging, averages the results of many classification trees from a series of bootstrapped samples (Lee, Lessler, & Stuart, 2010). In this procedure, a set number of participants are randomly sampled (with replacement) from the available dataset to estimate propensity scores using a CART procedure. Since CART automatically selects the covariates (and the order in which they are used in the model) based on their relative strength with the dependent variable, both the participants and covariates will vary for each CART model created from the bootstrapped sample. Cases that are not sampled are used to cross-validate the estimated model (Luellen, Shadish, & Clark, 2005). A separate classification tree is estimated for each bootstrapped sample, and the resulting trees are aggregated to create a single propensity score for each participant. Random forests are similar to bagging except that they randomly select the covariates that are tested in each model. In this approach, the researcher does not designate the specific predictor variables that will be in the model.

Like random forests, *machine learning* also uses a series of classification equations that are not based on a priori models, but are determined by testing available data for the best model fit. However, rather than randomly selecting covariates, some computer programs can create better classification and prediction models by repeatedly testing various combinations of variables (Lee et al., 2010; Linden & Yarnold, 2016; Westreich et al., 2010). Therefore, each successive model will fit the data better than the prior one. This iterative process continues until the classification model sufficiently predicts the dependent variable from the available predictor variables.

Boosted modeling, sometimes known as metaclassification, averages multiple PS models that were created using different combinations of covariates. Each model is weighted based on its ability to predict the assignment conditions and aggregated to form a single, stable model. Unlike bagging, it uses all available cases from the original sample for each model, and it weights cases based on how difficult they are to classify. When used with machine learning, higher weights are given to later models, since they are typically better models than previous models. Each individual prediction model can be estimated with either logistic regression or classification trees (Lee et al., 2010).

2.2d Which Method Is Best?

While PS estimates from logistic regression tend to perform well, other methods are also effective and may reduce bias better than those from logistic regression under certain conditions (Lee et al., 2010; Luellen et al., 2005; Setoguchi, Schneeweiss, Brookhart, Glynn, & Cook, 2008; Stone & Tang, 2013). For instance, when matching or stratifying on propensity scores, logistic regression tends to create better propensity scores than CART, boosted modeling, or bagging with less than 100 bootstrapped samples (Luellen et al., 2005; Stone & Tang, 2013). However, boosted modeling is often the optimal procedure to create propensity scores for weighting (Lee et al., 2010; Stone & Tang, 2013). CART estimates vary considerably depending on the specific CART model used. Therefore, when using CART, avoid "pruning" the classification trees and use it with random forests or boosted modeling (Lee et al., 2010; Setoguchi et al., 2008). Unfortunately, it is difficult to predict which will be the best PS estimator for any given set of data, since the results vary depending on the PS method (i.e., weighting, stratification, matching). When in doubt, your choices are logistic regression, CART (without pruning), and boosted modeling. Of these three, logistic regression is the easiest to use, which may explain its popularity among both substantive and methodological researchers. However, if you find that a single PS estimation using logistic regression or CART is not sufficient, it may be worth the extra effort to use boosted modeling.

2.3 Summary of the Chapter

For PS methods to effectively reduce selection bias, the propensity scores themselves must be good. This requires that we select appropriate covariates for the PS model and that they are modeled so that the PS distributions will accurately reflect the distributions of the covariates. When selecting covariates, it is important to consider how they are related to the treatment conditions and the outcome variables. In addition to including linear covariates in the PS model, you may also include nonlinear variables and interactions between covariates. Though probably less critical than the covariates chosen for the model, it is also important to consider which statistical algorithm will estimate the best propensity scores from these covariates. While some algorithms work better for certain adjustment methods than others, logistic regression and boosted modeling typically work well with most datasets.

2.4 An Example

In this section, we provide a description of the Playworks data used to demonstrate what we cover in Chapters 2, 3, and 4 and a demonstration on (a) how to select covariates for a PS estimation model and (b) the most commonly used methods for estimating propensity scores. Here, we provide only the statistics used to select covariates for the PS model. The specific procedures used to obtain these results with statistical software (e.g., R, STATA, SAS, and SPSS) are included on the companion website at **study.sagepub.com/researchmethods/qass/bai&clark**.

2.4a Description of the Data

The dataset that will be used to demonstrate the PS procedures throughout the book is a subset of the data that are publicly available from the Inter-University Consortium for Political and Social Research (ICPSR 35683). These data were collected from fourth- and fifth-grade students across six U.S. cities as part of the Playworks intervention program (www.playworks.org). The survey used to collect the data measured students' perceptions of the school climate, conflict resolution, learning and achievement, recess experience, and relationships with adults and peers. The subset of data selected for the examples in this book consists of 991 cases and 18 variables (listed in Table 2.2). The variables include one grouping (independent) variable (treatment vs. control), one outcome (dependent) variable, and 16 covariates. Those in the treatment group ($n = 147$) were assigned to

Table 2.2 Variables Selected for Demonstration in the Playworks Dataset

Domain	Construct	Variable Name (Levels)
Treatment Conditions (Independent Variable)	Assignment to Playworks	S_TREATMENT (comparison = 0, treatment = 1)
Outcome (Dependent Variable)	Student-reported feelings of safety at recess	S_CLIMATE_RECESSSAFETY
Covariates		
Demographics	Student gender	s_gender (female = 0, male = 1)
	Student grade	s_grade (Grade 4 = 4, Grade 5 = 5)
Perceptions of school climate	Sense of school as community	S_CLIMATE_COMMUNITY
	Student-reported feelings of safety at school	S_CLIMATE_SCHOOLSAFETY
Conflict resolution	Aggressive behavior	S_CONFLICTRES_AGGRESSIVE
	Relationships with other students	S_CONFLICTRES_RELATIONSH
	Normative beliefs about aggression	S_CONFLICTRES_AGGBELIEF
Learning, achievement, and classroom behavior	Effect of recess on behavior in class	S_LEARNING_RECESSEFFECT
	Effect of sports, games, and play on behavior in class	S_LEARNING_SPORTSEFFECT
	Engagement versus disaffection with learning	S_LEARNING_ENGAGEMENT
	Participation in organized games during recess	S_RECESS_ORGANIZED
	Enjoyment of recess	S_RECESS_ENJOYMENT
Youth development	Interactions with adults at school	S_YOUTHDEV_INTERACTIONS
	Self-efficacy for peer interaction: Conflict	S_YOUTHDEV_PEERCONFLI
	Self-efficacy for peer interaction: Non-conflict	S_YOUTHDEV_PEERNONCONFLICT
Physical activity and health	Physical activity self-concept	S_PHYSICAL_SELFCONCEPT

Playworks, a program in which elementary school playground coaches provided structure to a variety of activities that encourage engagement and conflict resolution. Those in the control group ($n = 844$) followed their existing recess activities without treatment interventions. Although the Playworks evaluation was originally designed as a group randomized trial, the subset of data that we use will mimic what one would find in a nonrandomized study. We would like to note that, since the cases are selected only for demonstration purposes, these data have limited empirical value with respect to any substantive research questions about the Playworks program.

2.4b Covariate Selection

As we described in Section 2.1, once we obtain the covariates that the literature suggests are related to the treatment conditions and the outcome, we can use statistical procedures to verify these relationships. Although it may be helpful to conduct preliminary tests using inferential statistics, final decisions about covariates that will be included in the PS model should be based on measures of standardized bias or effect sizes. Statistical tests, such as a *t*-test for continuous covariates and a chi-square test for categorical covariates, can be used to compare group differences as an initial reference. Correlations may be used to examine the relationships between the covariates and a continuous outcome. Commonly, a correlation between the covariates and the outcome that is greater than .1 indicates that the covariates are sufficiently related to the outcome, and an effect size (e.g., Cohen's *d*) larger than .05 or .1 suggests that the covariates distributed between the two comparison groups are not balanced. Using the Playworks data, Table 2.3 shows the relationships between all 16 covariates and both the treatment conditions and outcome. As you can see, all but three of these covariates (**S_CONFLICTRES_AGGRESSIVE, s_gender,** and **s_grade** as highlighted in bold) are biased based on Cohen's *d*, but when we examine the inferential tests, only seven covariates have significant differences between the treatment conditions. Using the more conservative criterion for Cohen's $d < .05$, we conclude that 13 of the covariates have bias that will influence the treatment effect. However, despite their initial balance, it is possible that these covariates will become unbalanced in the sample of matched data and hereafter influence the treatment estimation results. Therefore, we need to test on the balance status of all the covariates after PS adjustments.

Next, we check the correlations between the covariates and the outcome variable (S_CLIMATE_RECESSSAFETY). Among the continuous covariates, we found that neither S_YOUTHDEV_PEERCONFLICT nor S_YOUTHDEV_PEERNONCONFLICT are related to the outcome, but

Table 2.3 Relationships Between Covariates and Outcome Variable and Treatment Conditions

		Outcome[a]		Treatment Conditions[b]		
		r	χ^2/t	df	p (2-tailed)	d[c]
1	s_gender	0.05	.10[e]	1	.75	0.03
2	s_grade	0.02	.06[e]	1	.80	0.02
3	S_CLIMATE_COMMUNITY	0.55	7.96	808.40[d]	<.001	0.36
4	S_CLIMATE_SCHOOLSAFETY	0.79	1.95	989	0.052	0.17
5	S_CONFLICTRES_AGGRESSIVE	0.51	−0.73	526.09[d]	0.464	0.04
6	S_CONFLICTRES_RELATIONSHIPS	0.45	−1.43	989	0.153	0.13
7	S_CONFLICTRES_AGGBELIEF	0.48	−0.82	989	0.410	0.07
8	S_LEARNING_RECESSEFFECT	0.30	3.92	669.62[d]	<.001	0.19
9	S_LEARNING_SPORTSEFFECT	0.33	2.63	320.32[d]	0.009	0.16
10	S_LEARNING_ENGAGEMENT	0.39	1.62	989	0.105	0.15
11	S_RECESS_ORGANIZED	0.11	3.29	451.28[d]	0.001	0.18
12	S_RECESS_ENJOYMENT	0.20	1.82	718.75[d]	0.068	0.08
13	S_YOUTHDEV_INTERACTIONS	0.10	3.40	606.96[d]	0.001	0.17
14	S_YOUTHDEV_PEERCONFLICT	−0.01	2.67	989	0.008	0.24
15	S_YOUTHDEV_PEERNONCONFLICT	0.06	4.78	581.64[d]	<.001	0.24
16	S_PHYSICAL_SELFCONCEPT	0.10	0.97	989	0.332	0.09

Note: a. S_CLIMATE_RECESSSAFETY; b. s_treatment; c. Cohen's d; d. adjusted df when equal variance is not assumed; e = χ^2.

they are related to the treatment conditions. In this case, it is best to assume that the two variables could influence how Playworks impacts students' feelings of safety; therefore, we choose to include the two variables for the PS estimation model. Although S_CONFLICTRES_AGGRESSIVE has a weak relationship with the two treatment conditions, it has a strong correlation of 0.51 with the outcome variable. In this case, it could be beneficial to include this covariate in the PS model, especially since there is no limit to the number of covariates we can include in a PS model (Rosenbaum & Rubin, 1983), and accounting for aggressive behavior may reduce more bias.

On the other hand, the two categorical covariates, s_gender and s_grade, were not related to students' feelings of safety on the playground. Since these covariates are not associated with either the outcome or treatment conditions, we would normally exclude them from the PS estimation model. However, to demonstrate how both continuous and categorical variables can be used in PS models, we will include them in the examples we describe here and in Chapters 3 and 4.

2.4c Propensity Score Estimation

After determining which covariates are most likely to contribute to selection bias, we can estimate the propensity scores by modeling these covariates in a prediction model using the models described in Section 2.2. Although we demonstrate how to use classification trees and generalized boosted models (GBM) to estimate propensity scores on the book's website, here we use a logistic (or logit) model to demonstrate how to estimate propensity scores because it is more frequently used.

Estimating propensity scores using a logit model. Nearly all statistical software can be used to run a logistic model. When using a logistic (or logit) model to estimate propensity scores, the grouping variable (independent variable), which indicates the treatment conditions (e.g., S_TREATMENT in the Playworks dataset), has to be a binary variable (having only two categories).

Even though we used the outcome variable to determine which covariates to use, we should not include the outcome variable in our PS estimation model because the estimation of propensity scores should be independent of the outcome variable. Therefore, we ran a logistic regression in which Playworks participation (S_TREATMENT) was the dependent variable and all of our covariates (numbered from 4 to 19 in Table 2.4) were predictor variables. The predicted probability that each case (student) will be in the Playworks program is the propensity score. In general, when using analysis options specifically designed for computing propensity scores, an estimated propensity score for each case will be generated and saved at the end of the original data file. Table 2.4 includes a subset of the data used in our example to illustrate the values of the variables used in the PS model and the resulting propensity scores (in column 20: Pscore). From this table, notice that the propensity score for student (student_id) 2273 is 0.046, which is a composite score that represents all 16 covariates in columns 4 to 19. The estimated propensity score of 0.046 means that Student 2273, who is actually in the control group, has a 4.6% chance of being assigned to the treatment group based on his or her observed characteristics (i.e., the values of the 16 covariates).

Table 2.4 Estimated PS With the Values of the Covariates for Some Cases as an Example

1 student_id	2 S_TREATMENT	3 S_CLIMATE_RECESSSAFETY	4 s_gender	5 s_grade	6 S_CLIMATE_COMMUNITY	7 S_CLIMATE_SCHOOLSAFETY	8 S_CONFLICTRES_AGGRESSIVE	9 S_CONFLICTRES_RELATIONSHIPS	10 S_CONFLICTRES_AGGBELIEF	11 S_LEARNING_RECESSEFFECT	12 S_LEARNING_SPORTSEFFECT	13 S_LEARNING_ENGAGEMENT	14 S_RECESS_ORGANIZED	15 S_RECESS_ENJOYMENT	16 S_YOUTHDEV_INTERACTIONS	17 S_YOUTHDEV_PEERCONFLICT	18 S_YOUTHDEV_PEERNONCONFLICT	19 S_PHYSICAL_SELFCONCEPT	20 Pscore
2273	0	2.00	1	5	1.92	2.00	1.00	2.00	1.00	2.67	1.00	3.80	0.00	3.71	3.83	1.13	3.25	1.09	0.046
3973	1	2.75	0	4	2.77	2.25	1.50	3.33	2.38	1.67	2.67	3.50	2.50	3.86	3.83	2.25	2.00	1.82	0.094
5133	0	1.75	1	4	3.15	1.50	1.00	3.00	2.13	2.00	1.00	3.70	2.33	3.86	3.17	2.00	1.50	1.64	0.159
9834	0	1.75	0	4	2.92	1.75	1.67	3.67	1.57	3.00	3.00	2.70	2.00	3.71	3.33	1.63	1.25	2.00	0.133
13273	0	3.75	0	5	3.62	3.50	1.33	4.00	1.00	4.00	3.33	3.60	2.33	4.00	3.67	1.00	1.25	1.91	0.303
14973	1	3.00	1	5	3.31	2.00	2.17	2.33	1.88	1.67	2.67	2.80	1.67	3.71	3.50	2.38	2.00	1.55	0.279
16414	0	3.50	1	4	3.15	3.75	1.33	3.33	1.63	2.00	3.00	2.60	2.00	3.29	3.17	2.50	2.00	1.82	0.247
17974	1	2.75	1	5	2.92	2.50	1.00	3.00	1.75	2.33	2.00	3.00	1.67	2.71	2.50	2.75	2.00	1.27	0.203
18814	0	4.00	1	4	2.38	2.50	1.00	2.33	1.00	1.67	1.33	3.40	0.83	2.71	3.00	4.00	2.25	1.45	0.124
19444	0	2.00	0	5	2.33	1.75	1.00	−9.00	1.00	2.00	2.00	4.00	2.00	3.43	3.67	2.33	1.50	1.80	0.573

36

Now that we have the propensity scores for our sample, they can be used to evaluate the overall bias of the distributions of the covariates between the treatment and control groups and to implement the adjustment methods.

> **Checklist for Including a Covariate in the Propensity Score Model**
>
> ☑ The covariate is related to both treatment condition and outcome variable.
>
> ☑ The covariate is related to the outcome variable, but not the treatment condition.
>
> ☑ The covariate is related to the treatment condition and was measured (or manifested) before the treatment and has an impact on the treatment.

Study Questions for Chapter 2

1. What criteria should a researcher consider when selecting covariates to include in a PS model?

2. Using the *First Year Seminar* dataset (located at **study.sagepub.com/researchmethods/qass/bai&clark**), which of the available covariates have the strongest relationship with (a) the treatment condition (*Univ101*) and (b) the outcome variables (*FirstYrGPA* and *EnrollYr2*)?

3. What are some other potential covariates that are not available in the dataset that may influence selection bias when trying to estimate the effect that the first year seminar may have on academic performance?

4. Estimate the propensity scores from the *First Year Seminar* data using a logistic regression with

    a. Only covariates that are significantly related ($p < .05$) to the treatment condition (*Univ101*),

    b. Only covariates that are significantly related to college performance (*CollGPA*),

    c. Only covariates that are significantly related to both the treatment condition and college performance, and

    d. Covariates that are significantly related to either the treatment condition or college performance.

5. Estimate the propensity scores from the *First Year Seminar* data from all covariates that are significantly related to the treatment condition and college performance using

   a. the classification tree method and
   b. generalized boosted modeling.

How are the propensity scores different? Are they different from those in 4.d?

CHAPTER 3. PROPENSITY SCORE ADJUSTMENT METHODS

So far, we have discussed when to use PS methods and how to estimate propensity scores. Once propensity scores are created, researchers need to know how to use them. There are four commonly used methods in which we use propensity scores: matching, stratification, weighting, and covariate adjustment. This chapter will describe each of these adjustment methods and how they reduce selection bias. To demonstrate how these adjustment methods are used, we will continue to use the Playworks data as an example. At the end of this chapter, we present the results from two matching procedures. The course website provides the program codes, outputs, and interpretations for these matching procedures as well as for the other types of adjustment methods. By the end of this chapter, you should (a) be familiar with a variety of PS adjustment methods and (b) have a sense of how to select the most appropriate method based on your specific research design, set of data, and distributions of propensity scores.

3.1 Propensity Score Matching

PS matching pairs or groups cases in the treatment group to cases in the control or comparison group based on the proximity of their propensity scores. In this procedure, the propensity scores are a vector that serves as the matching variable. The matched cases result in a new dataset (selected from the original samples) that has similar distributions of propensity scores and covariates between the groups. PS matching is the most commonly used PS method for research within the social sciences, education, and medical science. Much like choosing an appropriate statistical procedure for computing propensity scores (see Chapter 2), it is also challenging to select an appropriate matching method or adjustment technique for similar reasons. Not only are there significant differences in how well PS matching methods reduce selection bias, but these differences may also depend on the distributions of the propensity scores. The first part of this chapter describes the most commonly used PS methods and when they are most efficient in practice.

3.1a Propensity Score Matching Typology

Like all PS methods, PS matching is used to improve internal validity by balancing the treatment and control or comparison groups on the observed covariates, which are related to the treatment and outcomes. However, matching is not exclusive to PS methods. It was used to improve causal inference in observational studies long before Rosenbaum and Rubin introduced propensity scores in 1983. While exact matching and Mahalanobis matching can be done with individual covariates, matching on propensity scores solves the problem of dimensionality that affects these classical matching algorithms (Guo & Fraser, 2015). Furthermore, it is often impossible to balance the treated and untreated groups on all covariates that affect selection bias when matching on individual covariates. Using a single score, such as the propensity score, makes it easier to find a good match from the control group for each treated case or group (Rosenbaum & Rubin, 1983). There are a variety of PS matching methods that can be summarized using a matching typology (Bai, 2013), which is illustrated in Figure 3.1. In the typology chart, the matching methods are classified into three categories: traditional matching, greedy matching, and complex matching. In general, types of greedy matching do not employ a global distance of the propensity scores between the matched pairs for the full set of cases to be selected, whereas the complex matching methods minimize the global distance of the propensity scores between the matched pairs among the selected cases. The matching typology in Figure 3.1 provides a guide for comparing and selecting the most appropriate matching method. Although Figure 3.1 contains 12 PS matching methods, we will focus only on the most efficient and commonly used ones: nearest neighbor, caliper, optimal matching, and full matching.

3.1b Greedy Matching

Nearest neighbor matching. Nearest neighbor matching matches each case in the treatment group (i) with a case in the control or comparison group (j) based on the closest absolute distance $d(i, j) = |l(Xi) - l(Xj)|$ between their propensity scores. There are several ways to conduct nearest neighbor matching. We can match a case in the treatment group to its nearest neighbor in the control group by ranking the propensity scores for both groups from largest to smallest or from smallest to largest, or match the cases in a random order. For example, we have a treatment group with propensity scores of .62, .74, .58, and .85 and a control group with propensity scores of .60, .36, .80, .74, .54, and .34. In this example, to use nearest neighbor matching without replacement, we should first rank both groups of propensity scores from largest to smallest: [.85, .74, .62, .58] for the treatment group and [.80, .74, .60, .54, .36, .34] for the control group, or from smallest to largest. Next, we start with the first case, which has a propensity score of .85, in the treatment group and find the propensity score in the control group with the

Figure 3.1 Matching typology

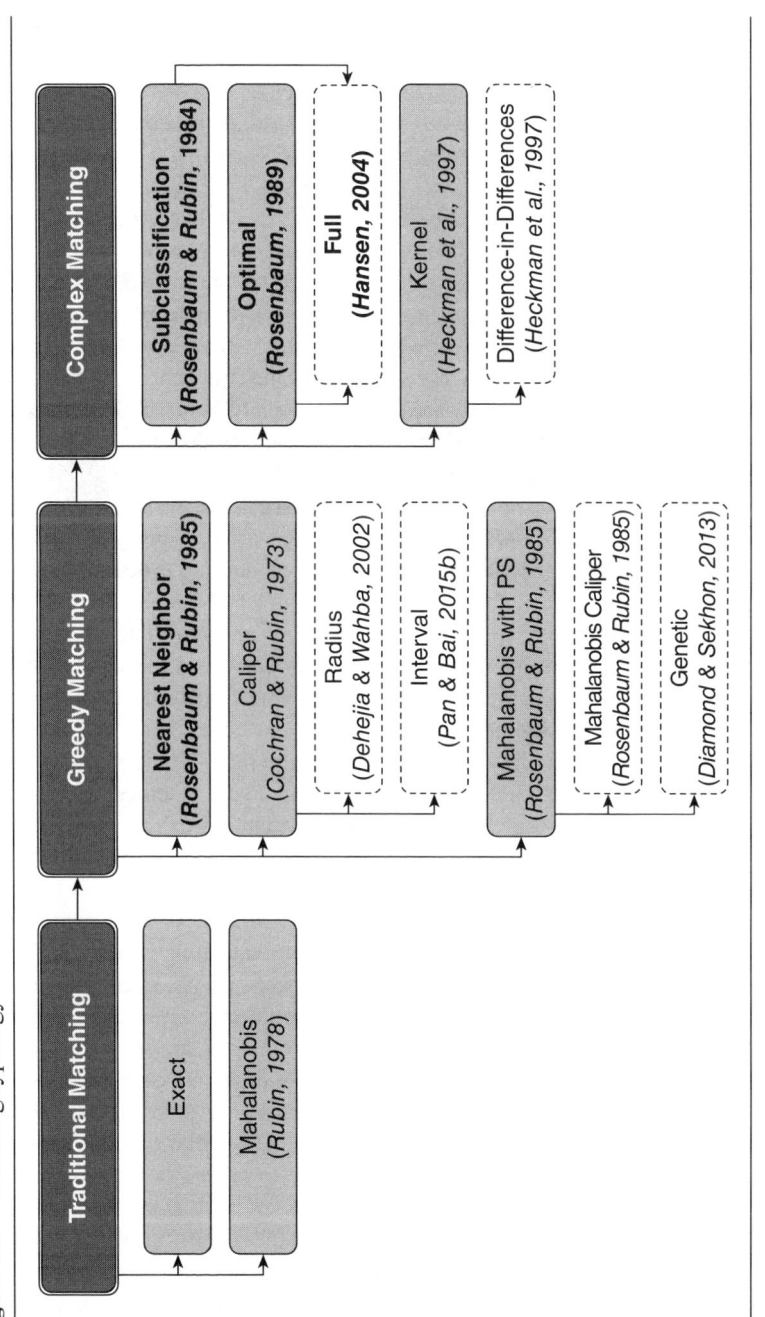

Note: Revised version based on Bai (2013).

closest value to .85, which is .80. Then we select them as a matched pair [.85, .80] to be included in the matched sample. We follow the same process to find a match for the second case, which has a propensity score of .74, in the treatment group. Since the closest number to .74 in the treatment group is .74 in the control group, the second pair is [.74, .74]. In the same fashion, we can find the remaining pairs, [.62, .60] and [.58, .54], in which .62 in the treatment group is matched with .60 in the control group, and .58 in the treatment group is matched with .54 in the control group. Even though both .62 and .58 (in the treatment group) are the same distance to .60 (in the control group), the control case with a propensity score of .60 can only be matched to one treatment case when matching without replacement. Since .62 is the higher value, the case with this propensity score was "greedily" matched first, so the control case with a propensity score of .60 is not available to pair with .58. Therefore, .54 is selected as the closest value from the remaining propensity scores in the control group to pair with .58 in the treatment group. Since there are only four cases in the treatment group, two of the six cases in the control group (i.e., those with propensity scores of .36 and .34) are not matched to cases in the treatment group. Because they have no matches, they are excluded from the new matched sample. Theoretically, the new sample should be balanced better on the covariate distributions between the two groups than the original sample. That is, members of the treatment and control groups will have similar characteristics except for their treatment conditions.

The example above presents the basic idea of nearest neighbor matching. In practice, however, there are two types of matching schemes. In the above example, we only demonstrate nearest matching *without* replacement. However, matching can also be done *with* replacement. Matching with replacement means that one case can be matched more than once. If a case in one group, either the treatment or control group, has a propensity score close to more than one case in the other group, matching with replacement allows a case to be selected more than once to pair with other cases. Using the above example, if we conduct matching with replacement, the case with a propensity score of .60 in the control group will be selected twice to match to cases with propensity scores of .62 and .58 in the treatment group, since .60 is closer to both .62 and .58 than all other values. Using this scheme, the final selected pairs are [.85, .80], [.74, .74], [.62, **.60**], and [.58, **.60**], and excluded cases in the control group are those with propensity scores of .34, .36, and .54.

Caliper matching. Caliper matching matches each case in the treatment group (*i*) to a case in the control group (*j*) within a predetermined caliper bandwidth (*b*). Cochran and Rubin (1973) recommend a $b \leq .25$ standard deviations of the matching variable to remove 90% of the bias. Following this criterion, Rosenbaum and Rubin (1985) recommended that the caliper bandwidth be no greater than .25 times the standard deviation of the propensity scores—that is, $b = .25 \times SD[p(X)]$. While this is a commonly used caliper, researchers may find that other bandwidths are more suitable for their particular sample of data. To apply caliper matching to our last example, we need to first find the standard deviation for the propensity scores of the treatment group [.85, .74, .62, .58], which is .12. Then, estimate the caliper width as $b = .25(.12) = .03$. Next, the first case, which has a propensity score of .85, has a bandwidth between .82 and .88 [.85 − .03; .85 + .03]. Unfortunately, there is no PS value in the control group that is between .82 and .88, so this treatment case is excluded from the matched data. Using caliper matching, the first case in the treatment group has no matched case in the control group. We can see that caliper matching is more restricted in its likelihood of finding matched pairs for all cases than are other forms of matching. The second pair is the same as what we found in nearest neighbor matching [.74, .74] because there is a case in the control group with the exact value. We find a matched score in the control group for the third case in the treatment group that falls within the caliper from .59 to .65 [.62 − .03; .62 + .03]. The only propensity score in the control group that falls within that interval is .60. Therefore, the second matched pair is [.62, .60], which is the same match that we used with nearest neighbor matching.

For Cases 2 and 3, matching with replacement would give us the same matches as matching without replacement. However, the best match for the fourth case in the treatment group would differ depending on the matching scheme. For a propensity score of .58, the caliper width is between .55 and .61 [.58 − .03; .58 + .03]. When we use matching with replacement, .60 is the closest match to .58. However, when we match without replacement, .60 is already paired with .62 and is no longer available. Therefore, .58 is left out of the matched sample because it cannot be matched to a control case. While this may not always be the case, in this sample, caliper matching with replacement permits more matched pairs ([.74, .74], [.62, .60], and [.58, .60]) than matching without replacement ([.62, .60] and [.74, .74]).

From the above example, which is also illustrated in Table 3.1, we can see that caliper matching will result in better matched pairs in terms of the values of their covariates. However, the number of matched pairs in the final sample might be significantly reduced; therefore, caliper matching is better suited for a large sample. An extensive discussion about bandwidth selection is beyond the focus of this book. Cochran and Rubin (1973) and Bai (2011) are good resources that address this topic more thoroughly.

Table 3.1 Comparison of Nearest Neighbor and Caliper Matching Methods With and Without Replacement

Original Sample		Nearest Neighbor				Caliper			
		Without Replacement		With Replacement		Without Replacement		With Replacement	
Treatment	*Control*	*Treatment*	*Control*	*Treatment*	*Control*	*Treatment*	*Control*	*Treatment*	*Control*
.85	.80	.85	**.80**	.85	**.80**				
.74	.74	.74	.74	.74	.74	.74	.74	.74	.74
.62	.60	.62	.60	.62	.60	.62	.60	.62	.60
.58	.54	.58	**.54**	.58	**.60**			**.58**	**.60**
	.36								
	.34								

Note: The values in the table are the propensity scores on which participants are matched. The values in bold are the control case matches that changed depending on the matching method used.

Other variants of greedy matching. There are other variations of greedy matching, including radius matching, interval matching, Mahalanobis matching with propensity scores, Mahalanobis distance matching with a caliper defined by propensity scores, and genetic matching. Since they are not widely used, we do not describe them in detail in this book; we only define the procedures and include related references for readers who are interested in learning more about them. Radius matching (Dehejia & Wahba, 2002; Huber, Lechner, & Steinmayr, 2015) is a variant of caliper matching that selects the nearest neighbor (the next closest case) within each caliper while using all the comparison cases within the caliper. Interval matching selects matched cases by identifying the overlapped confidence intervals of propensity scores for the cases from treatment and control groups using bootstrap confidence intervals to adjust the errors of PS estimation (Pan & Bai, 2015b). Mahalanobis matching with propensity scores (Rosenbaum & Rubin, 1985) matches the cases in the treatment and control groups using the Mahalanobis distance (Cochran & Rubin, 1973; Rubin, 1976, 1979, 1980), which is calculated from the covariates and the propensity score. Mahalanobis distance matching with a caliper

(Guo, Barth, & Gibbons, 2006; Rosenbaum & Rubin, 1985) matches the treated cases to the nearest neighbor (with cases in a random order) in the control or comparison group with the Mahalanobis distance within a caliper defined by the propensity score. Genetic matching uses a genetic search algorithm to minimize a multivariate weighted distance on covariates between treatment and control groups (Diamond & Sekhon, 2013).

3.1c Complex Matching

Optimal matching. Unlike greedy matching, optimal matching minimizes the global distance between propensity scores for all participants in the matched sample. Suppose we have a sample where the treatment group has propensity scores of .46, .29, .23, and .20, and the control group has propensity scores of .44, .42, .38, .38, and .27. If we use nearest matching, the matched pairs are [.46, .44], [.29, .27], [.23, .38], and [.20, .38]. As we can see, since nearest neighbor matching is greedy, the matching is done by selecting the best available unit to match the case without considering the collective matching quality of the final matched data. However, optimal matching considers every possible matched pair and selects the set of matches with the minimum overall differences in propensity scores between the groups. Therefore, for the above sample of data, optimal matching will result in the following pairs: [.46, .44], [.29, .38], [.23, .38], and [.20, .27], with the final global distance of $|.46 - .44| + |.29 - .38| + |.23 - .38| + |.20 - .27| = .33$, which is .04 smaller than the global distance from the nearest neighbor matching of $|.46 - .44| + |.29 - .27| + |.23 - .38| + |.20 - .38| = .37$. In general, optimal matching will provide better matches than nearest neighbor matching. However, if we have a large sample size or a substantial common support between the treatment and control groups, the results from optimal matching and nearest neighbor matching will be similar (Bai, 2015).

Full matching. Full matching selects samples to form subclasses that are matched to result in the minimum overall difference between propensity scores for the whole matched sample. These subclasses are created by finding one or more cases in the control group to match to one or more cases in the treatment group. Not all matched subsets need to include the same number of cases. That is, you can match either one case in the treatment group to one case in the control group, or one treated case to many control cases within the same matching procedure, or vice versa. Using the previous example in this section, we find that three cases in the treatment group have propensity scores (.20, .23, .29) that are closest to one case in the control group (.27), and four cases in the control group have propensity scores (.38, .38, .42, .44) that are closest to one case in the treatment group (.46). Therefore, instead of pairing one case in the treatment group to one case in the control group, we have clusters of varying sample sizes. The matched sample clusters or subclasses using full matching are [.20, .23, .29, **.27**] and [.46, **.44, .42, .38,** .38]. Full matching always allows matching with replacement and uses all cases, except the common support is set up prior to matching by removing some extreme values from both treated and nontreated cases. Full matching does not aim to create two distinct groups, because the purpose of full matching is to minimize a weighted average of the estimated distance between each treated case and each control case within each subclass (Ho, Imai, King, & Stuart, 2011). Therefore, the analytic model for estimating the treatment effect will need to weight observations from cases that were matched using this method. Table 3.2 shows how optimal and full matching compare with nearest neighbor matching in terms of the control cases that are selected as matches.

Other types of complex matching. As listed in the typology of PS matching methods (Figure 3.1), there are other types of complex matching methods that are not as frequently used as the methods we have just discussed. Although we will not describe them in detail, we would like to introduce these methods and provide sources for further information. Kernel matching uses a weighted average of all participants in the control group as a match for each participant in the treatment group

Table 3.2 Comparison of Nearest Neighbor, Optimal, and Full Matching Methods

| *Unmatched* || *Nearest Neighbor* || *Optimal* || *Full* ||
Treatment	*Control*	*Treatment*	*Control*	*Treatment*	*Control*	*Treatment*	*Control*
.46	.44	.46	.44	.46	.44		.44
.29	.42	.29	**.27**	.29	**.38**	.46	**.38**
.23	.38	.23	.38	.23	.38		**.38**
.20	.38	.20	**.38**	.20	**.27**	.29	**.27**
	.27					.23	
						.20	

Note: The values in the table are the propensity scores on which participants are matched. The values in bold are the control case matches that changed depending on the matching method used.

(Caliendo & Kopeinig, 2008). Difference-in-differences matching matches participants on changes in covariate bias from pretest to posttest (Heckman, Ichimura, Smith, & Todd, 1998).

3.1d Matching Variations

Matching with or without replacement. As discussed in the previous section, matching with replacement occurs when each case in the treated or nontreated group may be used as a match more than once. Matching without replacement limits each case to be matched with another only once. Unfortunately, it is unclear if or when PS matching should be done with or without replacement, as both schemes have their strengths and weaknesses.

Matching with replacement usually results in very different matched groups from matching without replacement; therefore, the matching method influences the accuracy of the treatment effect estimation. Matching with replacement usually produces better matches and reduces more bias than matching without replacement. Since matching with replacement places no restrictions on the availability of cases for matches, if a certain case in the control group is very similar to several cases in the treatment group, all of those treatment cases can be matched to that control case. Permitting cases to be matched to whichever case has the closest propensity score minimizes the global distance between the matched control treatment cases (Dehejia & Wahba, 2002). Matching without replacement is more likely to result in poor matches, especially if there are only a limited number of control cases that have propensity scores similar to those in the treatment group. Without reusing the same control cases, a treated case may be matched to a control case that has a very different propensity score, simply because there are so few good matches available in the control group.

A disadvantage in using matching with replacement is that we reduce the number of distinct cases in the control group that estimate the counterfactual mean, which may increase the variance of the estimator (Smith & Todd, 2005). Furthermore, matching with replacement reduces the independence between matched sets that contains the same treated or untreated cases, which must be accounted for when estimating the variance (Austin, 2011). Many of these issues can be avoided by using a control group with a large sample size, as this will prevent a large number of cases from being used multiple times. However, if the control group has a small sample size, matching with replacement may be more appropriate.

The choice to match with or without replacement should also be influenced by the type of PS matching method (e.g., nearest neighbor, caliper, optimal) and data conditions, such as the common support of PS distributions between the treated and untreated groups (Caliendo & Kopeinig, 2008). If there is good common support, matching without replacement may be less problematic; if not, matching with replacement could be a better choice (Dehejia & Wahba, 2002).

Ratio matching. Ratio matching is a way to assign multiple control cases to each treatment case. It is similar to full matching, in which each subset can have a varied number of treatment and control cases (e.g., we may have two treatment cases matched with three control cases or three treatment cases matched with one control case). However, ratio matching will match only one treatment case to a varied number of control cases (e.g., one treatment case matched with three control cases or one treatment case matched with two control cases). Of course, we can also have ratio matching in which several treatment cases are matched to one control case. This would be used if there were proportionally more treatment cases than control cases. Although a researcher can specify the maximum number of cases in one group that will be matched with each case in the other group, the resulting matches will not always have a consistent ratio. For example, if a researcher uses a 1 to 3 matching procedure, each treatment case will be matched to either 1, 2, or 3 control cases (depending on the distance of the matches). The number of cases in one group matched to each case of another group in ratio matching depends on the sample size ratio.

Sample size ratio. It is easier to find sufficient matches between the cases in the treatment and control groups when the sample size of the control group is considerably larger (e.g., three times as large) than the sample size of the treatment group (Rubin, 1979). However, a small sample size for a control group can still perform well with some of the PS matching methods, such as caliper matching with replacement (Dehejia & Wahba, 2002). With a large common support, the more available cases we have in the control group, the more likely we will find a match for those in the treatment group. However, varying the sample size ratio is not necessary if there is already good common support between the treatment and control groups (Bai, 2015).

3.1e Common Support

Sufficient common support between the treatment and control groups is one of the major assumptions for using PS matching methods. As we discussed in Chapter 1, common support is the overlap in the ranges of PS distributions of the treatment and control groups. When there is substantial overlap in the distributions of the propensity scores of the two groups (good common support), most of the matching algorithms yield similar results, and matching either with or without replacement is suitable. Violating the assumption of sufficient common support may not only prevent a sufficient reduction in bias, but may also affect external validity (Caliendo & Kopeinig, 2008; Heckman, Ichimura, & Todd, 1997). If the treatment and control groups do not yield similar values of propensity scores, they do not have the same characteristics; therefore, the groups are less likely to be samples from the same population. If we attempt to match cases with poor common support, most matching procedures will yield poor matches, which will not reduce the selection bias. Using caliper matching may ensure better matches, but it will likely exclude a substantial portion of the sample for analysis. If the only participants who are included in the analyses are those with propensity scores close to .5 (e.g., between .35 and .65), then we may not be able to generalize the treatment effect to those who are very likely or unlikely to receive the treatment.

Unfortunately, there is no standard criterion in the current literature for how much common support is sufficient for PS matching. We could follow Rubin's (2001) suggestion that the means of the group propensity scores should be less than .5 standard deviations apart. While this mean difference does provide some standard, it does not actually measure the range of common support or extent to which the propensity scores overlap between the groups. We can also use Caliendo and Kopeinig's (2008) minima and maxima comparison approach to trim the cases in the treatment group by excluding cases with propensity scores larger than the highest score in the control group, and trim the cases in the control group by excluding cases with propensity scores lower than the lowest score in the treated group. Although this method accurately measures the common support, it does not include a standard for how much common support is sufficient for PS matching. In the absence of a widely accepted standard, we recommend that 75% of the propensity scores overlap (Bai, 2015).

3.2 Other Propensity Score Adjustment Methods

3.2a Subclassification

Subclassification, also known as stratification or blocking, is a type of matching based on groups of cases. Like the matching methods described above, it attempts to balance covariates by matching treatment cases to control cases with similar propensity scores. However, rather than matching one treatment case to one or a few control cases, matches are made on intervals of propensity scores. Once propensity scores are estimated, the entire distribution of propensity scores is divided into strata, so that each stratum includes participants from the treatment and control groups.

Defining the strata. Two common approaches to creating strata are to create equal intervals based on (a) the PS ranges or (b) the proportion of participants. In the first method, the range of propensity scores is consistent across strata so that each stratum would be defined by a set interval of propensity scores depending on the number of strata. The second method creates intervals based on equal percentiles of the distribution of propensity scores. Participants would be rank ordered on the value of their propensity scores, and strata would be based on equal sample sizes or percentiles.

For example, suppose that we have 20 participants, whose propensity scores range in value from .07 to .89 and have a distribution like that shown in Table 3.3.

If we divide this distribution into four strata based on the ranges of propensity scores, the interval width or range would be .25, and each participant would be assigned to a stratum depending on his or her raw propensity

Table 3.3 Distribution of Propensity Scores

Propensity Score	Treatment Conditions
.07	control
.15	control
.19	treatment
.22	control
.26	control
.28	treatment
.31	control
.36	control
.36	treatment
.40	control
.41	treatment
.45	control
.48	treatment
.51	control
.54	treatment
.62	control
.65	treatment
.72	treatment
.77	treatment
.89	treatment

score. If our four strata were defined by the percentiles of the propensity scores, each stratum would include five cases or 25% of the sample, and cases would be assigned to strata based on their rank order. In either approach, participants in the treatment group would be matched to those in the control group in the same stratum. However, depending on the way that cut-points are defined, we may see very different matches for each participant. Table 3.4 illustrates how each stratification approach can be applied.

First, notice that many of the cases that were assigned to one stratum based on ranges are not assigned to the same stratum when using percentiles. This also means that matches will vary depending on the approach to defining strata. In our example above, the cases whose propensity scores are .41 and .48 are matched with cases whose propensity scores are .26, .31, .36, .40, and .45 using the first approach. However, they are matched with

Table 3.4 Subclassification Using Four Strata Based on Propensity Score Ranges and Percentiles

| | *Propensity Score Ranges* ||| *Propensity Score Percentiles* |||
Stratum	*Interval*	*Treatment*	*Control*	*Interval*	*Treatment*	*Control*
1	.00–.25	.19	.07	0–25th	.19	.07
			.15			.15
			.22			.22
						.26
2	.26–.50	.28	**.26**	26th–50th	.28	.31
		.36	.31		.36	.36
		.41	.36			.40
		.48	.40			
			.45			
3	.51–.75	.54	.51	51st–75th	**.41**	**.45**
		.65	**.62**		**.48**	.51
		.72			.54	
4	.76–1.00	.77		76th–100th	**.65**	**.62**
		.89			**.72**	
					.77	
					.89	

Note: The values in the table are the propensity scores on which participants are classified. The values in bold are the cases that are assigned to a different stratum depending on the criterion used to define the strata.

control cases whose propensity scores are .45 and .51 using the second approach. Second, in either approach there is not an equal number of participants from each group in each stratum (e.g., in Stratum 1, there is only one participant in the treatment group and three [strata defined by ranges] or four [strata defined by percentiles] participants in the control group). This is not unusual given that participants in the treatment group are more likely to select into the treatment group (and subsequently have greater propensity scores), and those in the control group tend to have lower propensity scores, reflecting their lower probability for choosing to be in the treatment group.

As you can see, one potential problem with subclassification is that some participants are not matched and would be dropped from the samples when estimating the treatment effect. While this is a common problem with other forms of matching, this can be reduced in subclassification by changing either the cut-points or the number of strata (Luellen et al., 2005). The former is illustrated in our example in Table 3.4. When strata are defined by ranges, there are no matches for the treatment cases whose propensity scores are .77 and .89. However, when strata are defined by percentiles, all cases are matched. While we may fail to find common support in a stratum when using either approach, this example shows how changing the cut-point can retain more cases in our analysis.

Varying the number strata. In our examples above, we divided our distribution into four strata. However, researchers may use either fewer than four or more than four strata. Reducing the number of strata increases the likelihood that all participants will be matched and included in the analyses. For example, if we used only two strata, all of the cases in the treatment group would be in strata that are matched with cases in the control group (see Table 3.5). Unfortunately, this also reduces the precision of the matches and the effectiveness in balancing the propensity scores. By increasing the interval, we can no longer discriminate between those who have propensity scores of .6 and .9. Therefore, this type of stratification may defeat the purpose of using PS methods. Increasing the number of strata will improve the similarity of the matched groups and the likelihood that groups are balanced on the propensity score (and subsequently the covariates). As the number of strata increases, the more subclassification looks like the matching methods discussed in Section 3.1 (e.g., full matching, in particular). The matches may improve with more strata, but we may also need to drop more participants from the analysis. Table 3.5 shows that if we divide our sample into six strata based on PS ranges, the proximity of the PS matches across groups is no greater than .14—as opposed to a difference of .22 when using four strata or .41 when using two. However, we would need to drop all control cases in Stratum 1 and all treatment cases in Strata 5 and 6, since they have no common support.

Table 3.5 Stratification Using Two and Six Strata Based on Propensity Score Ranges

	Two Strata			Six Strata		
Stratum	Interval	Treatment	Control	Interval	Treatment	Control
1	.00–.50	.19	.07	.00–.16		.07
		.28	.15			.15
		.36	.22			
		.41	.26			
		.48	.31			
			.36			
			.40			
			.45			
2	.51–1.00	.54	.51	.17–.33	.19	.22
		.65	.62		.28	.26
		.72				.31
		.77				
		.89				
3				.34–.50	.36	.36
					.41	.40
					.48	.45
4				.51–.67	.54	.51
					.65	.62
5				.68–.84	.72	
					.77	
6				.85–1.00	.89	

Note: The values in the table are the propensity scores on which participants are classified.

Cochran (1968) proposed that *five* strata created from percentiles could account for 90% of selection bias. However, using equal intervals based on percentiles was not optimal when using *more than five* strata. Although he found that increasing the number of strata tended to reduce more bias, bias reduction could be improved if the strata sample sizes were not equal. A better approach was to have a larger proportion of participants in the middle stratum (e.g., 30% in Stratum 3) and fewer participants in the lowest and highest strata (e.g., 10% in Strata 1 and 5).

Unfortunately, there is no correct or even best approach that can be generalized to all data samples. The best approaches in creating intervals for strata often depend on the distributions of propensity scores and the analytic approach. If the distributions of the propensity scores are very similar (i.e., there is a lot of common support or overlap between the distributions), then there will be little difference in the two methods for creating strata. However, if the distributions have little common support—either because the mean difference between the distributions of the group propensity scores is large or the PS distributions are skewed—the method for creating strata may be more influential. In these cases, it may be best to have many strata and drop the strata on the ends of the distributions. This method will be similar to the results found from matching on propensity scores. The matches will be precise, but you will drop several cases. To retain more cases, one may increase the interval widths on the strata with the highest and lowest propensity scores (i.e., Stratum 1 is the lowest 30% of the distribution and Stratum 5 is the highest 30%, while Stratum 3 is the middle 10% and Strata 2 and 4 each contain 15% of the distribution). If the PS distributions have heterogeneous variances (e.g., one is normally distributed and the other is skewed), creating strata based on percentiles may provide more balance across strata than basing them on PS ranges.

The biggest problem with subclassification is the trade-off between increasing the interval width of the strata to include more participants in the analysis and decreasing the interval width to obtain more precise matches. An advantage that stratification has over the matching methods described above is that by matching on groups, we can include more participants in each group that is matched. This reduces the likelihood that participants will be dropped from the analysis; however, it also reduces the precision of the match. This weakens the internal validity of the study, as participants are not as similar to each other as those in PS matching procedures described in the previous section on matching. Although matches can be improved by increasing the number of strata, this also increases the likelihood that some cases in one group will not have a comparable case in the other group (like what is shown for Strata 5 and 6 in Table 3.5). When there is a lack of common support, the participants without matches are dropped from the analysis, which weakens the external validity.

3.2b Weighting

Weighting balances treatment and control groups by multiplying the observations of the dependent variable by a weight based on the propensity scores. Although there are several PS weighting estimators

(Harder, Stuart, & Anthony, 2010; Hirano & Imbens, 2001; McCaffrey, Ridgeway, & Morral, 2004; Schafer & Kang, 2008; Stone & Tang, 2013), most of these methods weigh observations by the inverse of the propensity score. The most common PS weighting procedures (a) use the inverse probability of treatment weighted (IPTW) estimator to find the average treatment effect (ATE) or (b) weight by the odds to find the average treatment effect for the treated (ATT). The main difference between these procedures is that ATE adjusts the observations for all participants, while ATT only weights the observations of those in the comparison group. A common way to find the ATE is to weight the observations for the treated group by the inverse of the propensity score (see Equation 3.1) and the observations for those in the comparison group by the inverse of one minus the propensity score (see Equation 3.2).

So, for the treated group,

$$y_{wti} = \frac{y_{ti}}{e_{xi}}, \tag{3.1}$$

where y_{wti} is the weighted observation of the dependent variable for each participant in the treatment group, y_{ti} is the original observation for that participant, and e_{xi} is the propensity score for the comparison group,

$$y_{wci} = \frac{y_{ci}}{1-e_{xi}}, \tag{3.2}$$

where y_{wci} is the weighted observation for each participant in the comparison group and y_{ci} is the original observation for that participant. The weighted observations are then summed and divided by the total sample size (N). The difference between these averages is the average treatment effect (see Equation 3.3):

$$ATE = \frac{\sum_{i=1}^{n_t} y_{wti}}{n_t + n_c} - \frac{\sum_{i=1}^{n_c} y_{wci}}{n_t + n_c}, \tag{3.3}$$

where n_t is the sample size of the treatment group and n_c is the sample size of the control group.

The ATT can be found by weighting the observations of those in the treatment group by one (or not at all), and observations in the control group are weighted by the propensity score and the inverse of one minus the propensity score (see Equation 3.4):

$$y_{wci} = \frac{y_{ci}(e_{xi})}{1-e_{xi}}. \tag{3.4}$$

Unlike the ATE, the weighted observations are summed and divided by their respective sample sizes, n_t and n_c. The difference between these averages is the average treatment effect for the treated (see Equation 3.5):

$$ATT = \frac{\sum_{i=1}^{n_t} y_{ti}}{n_t} - \frac{\sum_{i=1}^{n_c} y_{wci}}{n_c}. \qquad (3.5)$$

Table 3.6 shows how each method is applied and how the results of these different weighting statistics can affect the treatment effect. When the observations are not weighted, the mean difference between the two conditions is .168 (.684 − .516). Using the ATE weights, the mean difference increases to .235 (.683 − .448) and the ATT is .304 (.684 − .380).

3.2c Covariate Adjustment

Covariate adjustment uses propensity scores as a covariate in an analysis of covariance (ANCOVA) or a multiple regression (Austin & Mamdani, 2006; Rosenbaum & Rubin, 1983). In simpler models, the propensity scores

Table 3.6 Comparison of ATE and ATT Weighting Results

Propensity Scores		Unweighted Observations		ATE Weighted Observations		ATT Weighted Observations	
T	C	T	C	T	C	T	C
0.2	0.1	0.36	0.39	1.80	0.43	0.36	0.04
0.3	0.2	0.53	0.28	1.77	0.35	0.53	0.07
0.4	0.2	0.44	0.42	1.10	0.53	0.44	0.11
0.4	0.3	0.67	0.33	1.68	0.47	0.67	0.14
0.5	0.3	0.62	0.47	1.24	0.67	0.62	0.20
0.5	0.4	0.82	0.55	1.64	0.92	0.82	0.37
0.7	0.4	0.76	0.64	1.09	1.07	0.76	0.43
0.7	0.5	0.91	0.58	1.30	1.16	0.91	0.58
0.8	0.5	0.85	0.78	1.06	1.56	0.85	0.78
0.9	0.6	0.88	0.72	0.98	1.80	0.88	1.08
Mean		0.684	0.516	0.683	0.448	0.684	0.380

Note: The means for the unweighted and ATT weighted observations are divided by the group sample sizes ($n = 10$), and the means for the ATE weighted observations are divided by the total sample size ($N = 20$).

are used instead of including covariates as individual predictors. Alternatively, doubly robust models include individual predictors in addition to propensity scores (Kang & Schafer, 2007). Therefore, covariate adjustment removes bias by accounting for the shared variance between the propensity scores and both the dependent variable and the treatment variable. Since the covariates that were used to model the propensity scores were also related to both the treatment condition and the dependent variable, the adjusted treatment effect should account for the bias from all of the covariates. Furthermore, since the propensity scores were modeled based on their relative importance to the treatment variable, the propensity scores will account for differential relationships between the covariates and dependent variables based on the treatment condition. In traditional covariate adjustment, the individual covariates will account for the shared variance between the dependent variable and treatment condition, but they may not account for how the treatment condition moderates the correlations between the covariates and the dependent variable. Therefore, traditional covariate analysis may not effectively balance the covariates between the treatment and control groups (Schafer & Kang, 2008).

Although several researchers have found that covariate adjustment can be an effective method for removing bias (Clark, 2015; Hade & Lu, 2013; Kang & Schafer, 2007), others have found that these results may not be valid under certain conditions. Therefore, it is important to consider the statistical assumptions when using regressions or ANCOVAs, such as linearity between the covariate and dependent variable or homogeneous group variances. Just as these assumptions are important in traditional covariate adjustments, they also affect the validity when using covariate adjustment with propensity scores. For example, bias may not be effectively reduced with this method when group variances among the covariates are heterogeneous (D'Agostino, 1998; Rubin, 2001). It also tends to be less effective when the functional form of the covariates used in the PS model is not linear (Hade & Lu, 2013). Rosenbaum (2010) also recommends that this method should be avoided if propensity scores are not linearly related to the dependent variable. However, this problem can be avoided by including nonlinear propensity scores as covariates in the adjustment model (Shadish et al., 2008).

3.3 Summary of the Chapter

Researchers typically use one of four PS adjustment methods: matching, stratification, weighting, and covariant adjustments with propensity scores. When used correctly, any of these methods can substantially reduce selection bias. Of these, matching is the most commonly used method among social and behavioral scientists. Matching often allows for the best comparisons between treatment and control groups, resulting in treatment estimates with strong internal validity. While it tends to exclude cases from the original sample of data, results from matching can be improved by using datasets with large sample sizes and proportionally more participants in the control or comparison group. Stratification is similar to matching, but by matching on groups of participants, we are less likely to exclude participants from the analyses. The drawback to this is that the matches are not as good; therefore, we may not reduce as much bias as a matching method with certain restrictions on common support or bandwidth. PS weighting can be applied to many data conditions, such as multilevel data or other complex data with latent variables or multiple treatment conditions. Unfortunately, weighting may not reduce selection bias as well as matching when propensity scores are skewed or include outliers. Covariate adjustment using propensity scores is the easiest method to use, but it is sensitive to the specific conditions of the propensity scores and covariates.

3.4 An Example

Although the details for how to implement propensity score methods using statistical packages (*R*, *SAS*, *STATA*, and *SPSS*) are described on the companion website, at **study.sagepub.com/researchmethods/qass/bai&clark** this section will show you what the results from those procedures look like. Here, we use the same treatment conditions, outcome variable, and 16 covariates to illustrate the results after applying propensity score methods that we used in Chapter 2 (see Table 2.2).

In the example in Chapter 2, we described how to estimate the propensity scores. However, many statistical packages will run the matching procedure along with the PS estimation. That is, you do not need two sets of procedures—both are run concurrently. In such cases, once you have specified the treatment (or grouping) variable (e.g., S_TREATMENT in the Playworks data) as the dependent variable and the covariates as the predictor variables, make your selections to specify your preferred matching procedure (e.g., matching with replacement, ratio matching, caliper width). For the following two examples, we have chosen to create our matched samples in *R* using (a) nearest neighbor, paired matching (1:1, where one case in the control group is matched to one case in the treatment group) without replacement; and (b) optimal, ratio matching (1:2, where one case in the treatment group is matched to two cases in the control group) without replacement. While results may vary slightly depending on the statistical package you use, the main results will be similar across packages.

Table 3.7 displays a subset of cases from the matched dataset after nearest neighbor matching. As you can see in Table 3.7, Student (student_id) 452513, who is in the comparison group and has a propensity score of

Table 3.7 Sample of Matched Cases After Nearest Neighbor Matching

student_id	S_TREATMENT	S_CLIMATE_RECESSSAFETY	s_gender	s_grade	S_CLIMATE_COMMUNITY	S_CLIMATE_SCHOOLSAFETY	S_CONFLICTRES_AGGRESSIVE	S_CONFLICTRES_RELATIONSHIPS	S_CONFLICTRES_AGGBELIEF	S_LEARNING_RECESSEFFECT	S_LEARNING_SPORTSEFFECT	S_LEARNING_ENGAGEMENT	S_RECESS_ORGANIZED	S_RECESS_ENJOYMENT	S_YOUTHDEV_INTERACTIONS	S_YOUTHDEV_PEERCONFLICT	S_YOUTHDEV_PEERNONCONFLICT	S_PHYSICAL_SELFCONCEPT	Pscore
1	2	3	4	5	6	7	8	9	10	11	12	13	14	15	16	17	18	19	20
678874	1	4.00	1	4	1.54	2.50	1.00	4.00	1.00	3.33	3.00	2.80	2.00	4.00	4.00	1.00	1.00	1.91	0.026
452513	0	2.75	1	5	1.23	1.50	1.67	3.00	1.13	2.67	4.00	3.30	2.67	3.71	2.17	1.25	1.00	1.91	0.026
380973	1	1.50	1	4	2.92	1.75	1.00	4.00	1.00	2.67	2.00	3.40	1.00	3.71	3.50	1.88	1.00	1.73	0.111
630850	0	1.75	1	4	2.77	2.25	1.83	3.33	2.38	2.00	2.33	3.00	2.17	3.71	3.67	2.50	1.75	1.73	0.114
553973	1	2.25	1	4	2.92	1.50	1.33	4.00	1.00	2.67	2.00	4.00	2.00	3.43	3.17	2.38	2.50	1.91	0.187
288417	0	3.00	0	5	3.00	2.50	1.17	3.33	1.00	2.33	3.67	2.80	2.17	4.00	3.00	1.63	1.25	2.00	0.187
901970	1	3.25	1	4	3.31	2.25	1.17	3.33	1.00	2.00	3.67	3.10	2.17	3.86	3.67	2.50	2.25	1.27	0.328
208174	0	1.25	0	4	3.23	1.50	1.00	2.67	2.50	2.67	2.67	2.60	2.00	3.29	3.83	3.43	3.25	1.73	0.329
428871	1	3.00	0	4	3.15	1.75	1.50	–9.00	1.00	2.00	4.00	3.00	1.67	3.86	4.00	1.00	1.00	1.91	0.762
683489	0	3.50	0	5	3.08	3.25	1.00	–9.00	2.50	2.67	2.33	2.60	1.33	3.71	2.83	1.75	2.75	2.00	0.768

59

0.026, was matched with Student 678874, who is in the treatment group and also has a propensity score of 0.026. This matched pair was determined by the similarity of their propensity scores, both of which are 0.026. While it is not necessary to have exact matches, as you can see from the table, another pair (Students 553973 and 288417) also is matched on exactly the same propensity score of 0.187, but the propensity scores for the other three pairs are not exactly the same. Since matching only selects the comparison cases that are most similar to the treatment cases, many of the control cases will not have matches and are not included in the matched samples.

Table 3.8 presents the sample sizes for each group before and after nearest neighbor matching. Since we did not use a caliper when matching, no cases in the treatment group were excluded from the matched sample. Therefore, the sample size in the full dataset ($n = 147$) is the same as that in the matched sample ($n = 147$). Since we used paired (1:1) matching, we selected 147 cases from the original sample in the comparison group ($n = 844$) to match with the treatment cases. Therefore, 697 cases in the comparison group are left unmatched and will not be used when estimating the effect that Playworks has on students' feelings of safety at recess.

Table 3.9 displays a subset of cases from the matched dataset after optimal matching. Since we used ratio matching (instead of paired matching), the output groups our matched cases into subclasses (Column 21) to identify which treatment and comparison cases are matched. In this example, 1:2 ratio matching gave us three cases in each subclass: one treatment case and two comparison cases. As you can see in Table 3.9, the first three cases all belong to Subclass 1, indicating that they comprise the first matched set. Students 818171 and 900043, both of whom are in the control group and have propensity scores of 0.280 and 0.279, respectively, are matched with Student 14973, who is in the treatment group and has a propensity score of 0.279. As in the previous example, these cases are matched based on the proximity of their propensity scores, so the propensity scores within each subclass are very similar.

Table 3.8 Sample Sizes Before and After Paired, Nearest Neighbor Matching

	Control	*Treated*
All	844	147
Matched	147	147
Unmatched	697	0

Table 3.9 Sample of Matched Cases After Optimal Matching With Their Propensity Scores

1	2	3	4	5	6	7	8	9	10	11	12	13	14	15	16	17	18	19	20	21
student_id	S_TREATMENT	S_CLIMATE_RECESSSAFETY	s_gender	s_grade	S_CLIMATE_COMMUNITY	S_CLIMATE_SCHOOLSAFETY	S_CONFLICTRES_AGGRESSIVE	S_CONFLICTRES_RELATIONSHIPS	S_CONFLICTRES_AGGBELIEF	S_LEARNING_RECESSEFFECT	S_LEARNING_SPORTSEFFECT	S_LEARNING_ENGAGEMENT	S_RECESS_ORGANIZED	S_RECESS_ENJOYMENT	S_YOUTHDEV_INTERACTIONS	S_YOUTHDEV_PEERCONFLICT	S_YOUTHDEV_PEERNONCONFLICT	S_PHYSICAL_SELFCONCEPT	Pscore	subclass
14973	1	3.00	1	5	3.31	2.00	2.17	2.33	1.88	1.67	2.67	2.80	1.67	3.71	3.50	2.38	2.00	1.55	0.279	1
818171	0	3.00	0	4	3.38	3.25	1.50	3.67	2.00	2.33	3.67	3.10	2.33	3.43	2.83	2.75	2.75	1.45	0.280	1
900043	0	3.00	1	5	2.77	1.50	1.00	2.67	1.00	2.67	1.67	4.00	0.50	1.14	3.67	3.50	3.75	1.45	0.279	1
145853	0	3.00	1	5	2.31	2.00	1.00	3.67	1.00	3.00	2.33	3.50	1.83	3.86	3.50	3.00	2.00	1.64	0.110	2
172976	1	2.75	0	4	2.92	1.75	1.00	3.67	1.00	2.33	3.00	3.70	1.00	4.00	3.67	1.50	2.25	1.55	0.110	2
308131	0	1.25	0	4	3.00	1.75	1.33	3.33	2.25	1.67	2.00	4.00	2.67	3.57	4.00	2.50	1.00	2.00	0.109	2
690973	1	3.50	1	4	2.69	2.25	1.00	3.33	1.63	2.67	3.33	2.90	1.83	4.00	2.17	1.88	1.75	1.73	0.130	3
757614	0	2.00	0	5	2.38	1.00	1.33	2.67	1.63	2.67	3.67	3.20	2.33	4.00	3.50	2.75	2.25	1.73	0.130	3
844453	0	3.50	0	4	2.85	3.25	1.17	2.67	2.50	3.00	2.67	2.80	1.17	3.57	2.67	2.38	2.50	1.64	0.130	3
705970	1	2.50	0	5	2.23	2.25	1.17	2.00	2.63	2.67	1.67	2.90	2.00	3.86	2.17	2.75	2.50	1.73	0.082	4
825610	0	2.25	1	5	2.31	1.00	1.67	3.00	2.13	2.33	2.00	2.60	2.67	3.86	4.00	2.00	1.00	2.00	0.083	4
876274	0	2.25	0	5	2.62	2.00	1.17	2.67	2.38	2.00	2.33	3.10	1.00	3.29	2.50	1.75	2.50	1.64	0.083	4

Table 3.10 Sample Sizes Before and After Optimal, Ratio (1:2) Matching

	Control	Treated
All	844	147
Matched	294	147
Unmatched	550	0

Table 3.10 presents the sample sizes for each group before and after optimal matching. Having used 1:2 ratio matching, the sample size of the control group in the matched dataset ($n = 294$) is twice as large as that for the treatment group ($n = 147$). Therefore, out of the original comparison group sample ($n = 844$), 550 cases are left unmatched and will not be used to estimate the treatment effect.

While this particular set of data was suitable for both paired and ratio matching, ratio matching may not be a good procedure if the comparison group has a small sample size. Therefore, prior to using this method, examine the ratio of the sample sizes to make sure that there is a sufficient number of cases in the control group. It should be at least k times more than the treatment group. In this example, we had 147 cases in the treatment group and 844 cases in the comparison group, which is far more than twice the sample size of the treatment group ($n = 294$). However, if there had been only 200 available cases in the comparison group, the ratio matching program might have failed to run. If our sample had more treated cases (e.g., $n = 2,000$) than comparison cases, ratio matching could still be used, but we would match multiple treated cases to a single control case.

It is also worth noting that in the example here, we matched cases without discarding any of the treated cases. However, some datasets might have outliers in either the control or treatment group or treatment cases that are far beyond the common support of the comparison group. In this situation, researchers can choose to remove these outliers (usually multivariate outliers) before estimating the propensity scores or use some relevant PS adjustment, such as caliper matching, to obtain more comparable pairs. With that being said, you may see that some cases in either the treatment or the control group may be removed from the final matched sample.

Although we limited our examples here to the results from only two matching methods, the book's website includes detailed demonstrations on how to use R, SAS, STATA, and SPSS to conduct these and other types of PS methods (e.g., full matching, caliper matching, matching with replacement, subclassification, weighting, and covariate adjustment with propensity scores). We will discuss how to evaluate the results from the matched sample (i.e., balance of the covariates' distributions) in Chapter 4.

Checklist for the Common Support of the Propensity Scores

- ☑ If you graph the distributions of the propensity scores, do the distributions appear similar in terms of the shape, mean, and minimum and maximum values?

- ☑ If you compute the minimum and maximum values of the comparison group, does at least 75% of the cases in the treatment group also fall in that range?

- ☑ If you compute a standardized mean difference (i.e., Cohen's d) of the propensity scores between the groups, is this value less than .5?

- ☑ If you compute an inferential test (i.e., t-test or chi-square test) to compare the propensity scores between the groups, are the groups significantly different?

Study Questions for Chapter 3

1. What are the most common PS methods?
2. How are matching methods (nearest neighbor, caliper, optimal, and full) different from each other?
3. When might you want to use
   a. sampling with replacement instead of sampling without replacement?
   b. full or ratio matching instead of paired matching?
   c. a sample with more control cases than treatment cases?
4. Using the *First Year Seminar* dataset (located at **study.sagepub.com/researchmethods/qass/bai&clark**), compute propensity scores using all 10 covariates and match students who participated in the first year seminar (*Univ101* = 1) to those who did not (*Univ101* = 0). Using paired (1 to 1) matching without replacement, how do the matches change when you use
   a. nearest neighbor matching?
   b. caliper matching (with a caliper width of .25)?
   c. optimal matching?

5. Using the same propensity scores from Question 4, match students who participated in the first year seminar to those who did not using
   a. full matching.
   b. nearest neighbor matching with replacement.
   c. nearest neighbor matching with ratio matching, in which every person in the treatment group is matched with two people in the control group (1:2).
   d. optimal matching with ratio matching, in which every person in the treatment group is matched with two people in the control group (1:2).
6. If you had to select one of the matching methods you used in Questions 4 and 5, which would it be? Why?

CHAPTER 4. COVARIATE EVALUATION AND CAUSAL EFFECT ESTIMATION

When applying PS methods, it is important to know the balance of the covariate distributions before and after the PS adjustment procedures. Since the main purpose of the PS methods is to reduce the selection bias through balancing the covariate distributions, it is essential for a researcher to know if a covariate is contributing to selection bias. Knowing the status of covariate balance (i.e., whether it is balanced or not) prior to estimating the propensity scores allows a researcher to know whether or not a covariate needs to be included in the PS model. Knowing this after the PS procedure tells the researcher whether or not he or she needs to modify the PS model, use a doubly robust procedure when estimating the treatment effects, or just estimate the treatment effects based on the adjustments discussed in Chapter 3. Therefore, in this chapter, we will begin by discussing how to evaluate the effectiveness of the PS methods in terms of their ability to balance covariates. Next, we will discuss how to estimate the treatment effects using the PS methods and determine whether or not these effects are robust. At the end of the chapter, we will use the Playworks data to demonstrate how these procedures can be applied using statistical software. The book's website provides the program codes, outputs, and interpretations for the outputs from a variety of statistical packages. By the end of this chapter, you should know (a) how to evaluate the balance of covariate distributions, (b) how to estimate an adjusted treatment effect, and (c) how to assess the sensitivity of the treatment effect estimate to hidden bias.

4.1 Evaluating the Balance of Covariate Distributions

Before PS matching, it is essential to check the balance of all of the observed covariates to see which ones are contributing to the selection bias. Distributions of covariates are likely balanced if there is no relationship between the treatment conditions and the covariates or no relationships between propensity scores and the covariates (Rosenbaum & Rubin, 1984). If the groups are well balanced on all covariates, there is no need to conduct any matching or weighting procedures; however, it is unrealistic to expect this outcome. While there are some nonrandomized studies that are not affected by selection bias, many of them are. Therefore, it is important to gauge how much the treatment effect is influenced by bias and which covariates need to be balanced. However, it is more important to check covariate balance after using a PS method, because it is often the case that some covariates are still not well balanced after matching; in some instances, matching may even increase covariate imbalance (King & Nielsen, 2016). When checking covariate balance, include covariates that were *not* used to compute propensity scores as well as those that were, as it is possible that covariates that were balanced before the PS method may not be balanced after the adjustment. In situations where covariates are still not balanced after the PS adjustment, researchers should implement further procedures to adjust the unbalanced covariates, such as a doubly robust procedure (Schafer & Kang, 2008). In the following sections, we introduce the three most commonly used criteria for assessing covariate balance between the treatment and comparison groups.

4.1a Selection Bias

The most basic technique for assessing the selection bias (B_k) associated with a covariate X_k, where $k = 1, \ldots K$, is to find the mean difference in the covariate between the treatment conditions. That is,

$$B_k = M_{1(X_k)} - M_{0(X_k)}, \tag{4.1}$$

where $M_{1(X_k)}$ is the mean of the covariate for all the cases in the treatment group and $M_{0(X_k)}$ is the mean of the covariate for those in the control group before PS adjustment. After the adjustment, $M_{1(X_k)}$ represents the mean of the treatment group and $M_{0(X_k)}$ is the mean of the control group only for those cases selected after the adjustment.

For example, suppose that we are worried that our treatment and comparison groups are not balanced on age. We may first assess the mean differences in age between the groups prior to matching and again after matching. Tables 4.1 and 4.2 illustrate how this can be done using an initial sample of 20 participants (10 in each condition) and a matched sample of 12 (6 in each condition). Prior to matching (Table 4.1), the mean age for the treatment group was 40 and the mean age of the comparison group was 35. Therefore, the selection bias is 5 ($B_k = 40 - 35$). However, after matching on the propensity score, the mean age for the treatment group is 39 and the mean age of the comparison group is 38.14, making $B_k = 0.86$.

To evaluate the extent of the selection bias, inferential tests can be used in which the treatment condition is the independent variable and the covariate is the dependent variable. Typically, an independent-samples t-test is used for continuous covariates and a chi-square (χ^2) test is used for categorical covariates (Bai, 2013). However, inferential tests should only be used in conjunction with other balance-checking methods, since the aim of the

Table 4.1 Full Sample Before Matching on Propensity Scores

Treatment Group			Comparison Group		
Participant	Propensity Score	Age	Participant	Propensity Score	Age
A	0.19	27	K	0.07	25
B	0.28	28	L	0.15	27
C	0.36	45	M	0.22	24
D	0.41	34	N	0.26	40
E	0.48	35	O	0.31	31
F	0.54	41	P	0.36	23
G	0.65	63	Q	0.4	41
H	0.72	32	R	0.45	37
I	0.77	38	S	0.51	53
J	0.89	57	T	0.62	49
Mean	0.529	40	Mean	0.335	35
SD	0.23	11.95	SD	0.17	10.70

Table 4.2 Sample After Matching Pairs on Propensity Scores

Treatment Group			Comparison Group		
Participant	Propensity Score	Age	Participant	Propensity Score	Age
A	0.19	27	M	0.22	24
B	0.28	28	N	0.26	40
C	0.36	45	P	0.36	23
D	0.41	34	Q	0.40	41
E	0.48	35	R	0.45	37
F	0.54	41	S	0.51	53
G	0.65	63	T	0.62	49
Mean	0.416	39	Mean	0.403	38.14
SD	0.16	12.40	SD	0.14	11.41

test is to measure the magnitude of the covariance balance in the sample, not to make inferences to the population, which may be affected by sample size and variance (Pan & Bai, 2016).

4.1b Standardized Bias

Because the selection bias addresses only the differences between the two group means of the covariate, it cannot fully represent the two distributions. Therefore, it is better to consider the results from other statistics as well. A measure of standardized bias (*SB*) (Rosenbaum & Rubin, 1985) is a more commonly used statistic, as it measures the mean difference relative to the variability of the values in the covariate distribution. This measure is very similar to Cohen's *d*, an effect size used to measure the difference between group means. Because *SB* and *d* are used to measure the magnitude of differences in a sample, rather than make inferences to a population, they are less dependent on the sample size. Both *SB* and *d* are standardized mean differences, which are estimated by dividing the difference in means between two groups (B_k) by the pooled standard deviation. While both are used to estimate selection bias, *SB* differs from *d* in that it multiplies the standardized mean difference by 100:

$$SB = \frac{B_k}{\sqrt{\frac{V_{1(X_k)} + V_{0(X_k)}}{2}}} \times 100\% \quad (4.2)$$

where $V_{1(X_k)}$ represents the variance of the covariate for the treated cases and $V_{0(X_k)}$ represents the variance for control cases. Using the same samples in Tables 4.1 and 4.2, the standardized bias of the unmatched samples is 44.1% [*SB* = (5/11.34)100], and the standardized bias of the matched samples is 7.2% [*SB* = (.86/11.94)100].

For binary categorical variables, the standardized bias is the difference between the proportions of a characteristic in each of two groups divided by the pooled standard deviation and multiplied by 100 (Austin, 2009). Mathematically, this can be expressed as

$$SB = \frac{\hat{P}_T - \hat{P}_C}{\sqrt{\frac{\hat{P}_T(1-\hat{P}_T) + \hat{P}_C(1-\hat{P}_C)}{2}}} \times 100\% \quad (4.3)$$

where $\hat{P}_T$ and $\hat{P}_C$ denote the proportion of the sample with a certain characteristic in the treatment and the control groups, respectively. For example, if 6 out of 10 people in the treatment group were females, $\hat{P}_T = .6$ and 4 out of 10 people in the comparison group were females, $\hat{P}_C = .4$, the pooled standard deviation would be .49 and the standardized bias would be 40.8% {*SB* = [(.6 − .4)/.49]100}.

In the above formulas, the sample means, variances, and proportions are unweighted estimates. However, if PS weighting is used, the weighted estimates should be used to assess covariate balance after PS weighting. The weighted mean would be $\bar{x}_{weight} = \dfrac{\sum w_i x_i}{\sum w_i}$, where w_i is the weight assigned to each case and x_i is the value of the covariate for each case, and the weighted sample variance is $s^2_{weight} = \dfrac{\sum w_i}{\left(\sum w_i\right)^2 - \sum w_i^2} \sum w_i \left(x_i - \bar{x}_{weight}\right)^2$ (Harder et al., 2010).

For example, suppose that we used 1 to 2 ratio matching procedure in which each treatment case is matched with as many as two control cases; we may give some of the comparison cases different weights like those shown in Table 4.3. In this example, the weighted mean age for the treatment group is still 39, but the weighted mean age for the comparison group is 37.73. These are obtained by multiplying each age value by its corresponding weight, summing the weighted ages, and dividing the sum by the weighted sample size, which is the sum of the weights. Selection bias is 1.27, which is the difference in the weighted means (B_k = 39 – 37.73), and the standardized bias is .107, which is the difference in the weighted means divided by the pooled standard deviation of the unweighted values (SB = 1.27/11.87). See Section 4.2a below for more on assigning weights when matching on propensity scores.

Table 4.3 Sample After Ratio Matching on Propensity Scores

	Treatment Group			*Comparison Group*				
Participant	*Propensity Score*	*Age*	*Weight*	*Participant*	*Propensity Score*	*Age*	*Weight*	*Weighted Age*
A	0.19	27	1	L	0.15	27	.64	17.28
				M	0.22	24	.64	15.36
B	0.28	28	1	N	0.26	40	.64	25.60
				O	0.31	31	.64	19.84
C	0.36	45	1	P	0.36	23	1.29	29.67
D	0.41	34	1	Q	0.4	41	1.29	52.89
E	0.48	35	1	R	0.45	37	1.29	47.73
F	0.54	41	1	S	0.51	53	1.29	68.37
G	0.65	63	1	T	0.62	49	1.29	63.21
Weighted Mean		39						37.73

A clear advantage for using the standardized bias over other methods is that it considers the variability of covariate scores but is influenced by the sample sizes less than an inferential statistic. Unfortunately, there is no clear standard for what we may consider to be a "balanced" covariate. Kang and Schafer (2007) recommend $SB < 40\%$, Harder et al. (2010) recommend $SB < 25\%$, and Caliendo and Kopeinig (2008) recommend $SB < 5\%$. We consider that a SB that is greater than 20% suggests poor balance, and the first two criteria are too liberal. For those who consider $SB < 5\%$ to be too conservative, requiring that SB be less than 10% may be acceptable.

4.1c Percent Bias Reduction

The percent bias reduction (PBR) is another commonly used method to check the balance of covariates between the treatment and control groups. Cochran and Rubin (1973) suggest that methods that can reduce bias by 80% or more are effective. The percent bias reduction is defined as (Bai, 2010)

$$PBR_k = \frac{|B_{before\,matching}| - |B_{after\,matching}|}{|B_{before\,matching}|} \times 100\% \qquad (4.4)$$

where $B_{before\,matching}$ denotes the selection bias before matching and $B_{after\,matching}$ is the selection bias after matching. The PBR is the ratio of the absolute value of the difference between the bias before and after matching divided by the bias before matching. Using the data in Tables 4.1 and 4.2, we found that the selection bias for age was 5 before matching and .86 after matching. Therefore, the percent bias reduction is 82.8% $\{PBR_k = [(5 - .86)/5]100\}$. If the SB estimate does not reach the benchmark, but the PBR is high (i.e., $PBR > 80\%$), the propensity scores are still considered to be effective in reducing bias; however, researchers may want to use a doubly robust method, in which covariates are added as an individual covariate.

4.1d Graphs and Inferential Tests

Graphs. Graphs are also good alternatives for assessing the balance of the distributions of covariates; some of these may include Q-Q plots, histograms, and love plots (Ahmed et al., 2006; Cochran & Rubin, 1973; Pan & Bai, 2015a; Pattanayak, 2015; Rosenbaum & Rubin, 1985). Most statistical software allows researchers to easily produce these graphs. Some software packages automatically check for covariate balance as part of the matching procedures (e.g., MatchIt in R) (Ho et al., 2011). The example at the end of the chapter illustrates a few of these graphs and how to interpret them.

Inferential tests. Hotelling's T^2 is an inferential test used to measure global covariate imbalance by testing the equality of means for all continuous covariates simultaneously. Like the measures of selection bias and standardized bias, it is based on the difference between means without considering the shape of the covariates' distributions. Therefore, researchers (Gilbert et al., 2012; Sekhon, 2008) recommend using the two-sample Kolmogorov-Smirnov test to compare the covariate distributions between the two groups. The null hypothesis is that both groups have identical distributions for the covariates. Therefore, it tests for differences in the group medians, variances, and cumulative distributions of covariates in addition to mean differences.

Even though inferential tests such as *t*-tests, chi-square tests, Mantel-Haensel tests, and Kolmogorov-Smirnov tests may be used to assess the statistical significance of the imbalance of measured covariates, they should be used with caution, as changes in balance may be conflated with changes in statistical power (Ho et al., 2011).

4.2 Causal Effect Estimation

Causal effect estimation with PS methods can be classified into two major procedures: (a) treatment estimation after PS matching, and (b) the treatment effect estimation with PS weighting to adjust the selection bias. This section will focus on the variety of statistical models for treatment effect estimation after implementing different PS matching strategies and briefly introduce PS weighting as an adjustment for treatment effect estimation.

4.2a Analyses After Matching

Once matches are made, a variety of statistical analyses can be used to estimate the treatment effects. If a paired greedy matching procedure (e.g., nearest neighbor) is used to match cases, a traditional univariate or multivariate statistic may be used to compare groups on the outcome. However, if matches are made using a complex procedure (e.g., optimal, full, or ratio matching), more complex analyses are needed to account for the lack of independence within group observations (Guo & Fraser, 2015).

Treatment effects can be estimated using a between-subjects analysis (e.g., independent samples *t*-test) or a within-subjects analysis (e.g., paired samples *t*-test) if the matched groups are substantially well matched. Both theoretical and applied arguments have been made for each type of analysis (Leite, 2017). Because cases are matched on several characteristics, it is theoretically sound to treat the matched cases as related observations and use a within-subjects analysis. Since the participants are matched on an aggregate covariate (the propensity score), the characteristics of the individuals will be more similar to each other than if they were randomly selected or assigned to conditions. Austin (2011) found that a within-subjects analysis on matched cases provided more accurate results than the between-subjects analysis, albeit the differences were small. Assuming that propensity scores meet the assumptions discussed in Chapter 1, an advantage in using within-subjects analyses is that these equations tend to estimate smaller error variances than between-subjects analyses and may provide more statistical power. However, this approach may not provide consistent results if propensity scores are computed from a few variables or do not include all covariates that influence selection bias.

Because we are not comparing the same participants or may not match them on a sufficient number of characteristics, others have argued that it may be more suitable to treat those in the treatment and control groups as independent observations. While the distributions of the propensity scores may be similar between groups, the covariates themselves are not the same (Stuart, 2010). Furthermore, Schafer and Kang (2008) argued that the outcomes of matched individuals are unlikely to be correlated (p. 298), in which case matching would not warrant using a within-subjects analysis. A likely conclusion to these arguments may be that the preferred analytic approach should depend on the number and quality of the covariates used to construct the PS model, the balance of the covariates after the matching procedure, and the correlation between the matched cases on the outcome variables.

Analyses for paired matching. Simpler designs allow for simpler analysis. Therefore, if one-to-one matching without replacement was done using an optimal or greedy approach (i.e., nearest neighbor matching with or without a caliper), treatment effects can be estimated using standard univariate or multivariate analysis.

Between-subjects analyses may include the following:

- An independent samples t-test, one-way analysis of variance (ANOVA), or ordinary least squares regression when comparing groups on a single continuous outcome variable

- A multivariate analysis of variance (MANOVA) (e.g., Hotelling's T or Wilks's lambda) when comparing groups on several continuous outcome variables

- A chi-square test of association or multinomial logistic regression when comparing groups on a single categorical outcome variable

- A logistic regression when comparing groups on a single dichotomous outcome variable

Within-subjects analyses may include the following:

- A paired samples t-test, repeated measures ANOVA, or regression adjustment used with difference scores (Rubin, as cited by Guo & Fraser, 2015) when comparing groups on a single continuous outcome variable
- A repeated measures MANOVA (e.g., Hotelling's T or Wilks's lambda) when comparing groups on several continuous outcome variables
- A McNemar's test when comparing two groups on a single dichotomous outcome variable

Analyses for complex matching. If matching was done with replacement or using ratio or full matching, treatment estimates must accommodate unequal sample sizes or lack of independence within observations. Between-subjects analyses are similar to the ones used with paired matching, but observations are weighted. For example, an independent samples t-test may still be used when comparing groups on a single continuous outcome variable, but only after observations are weighted. The weights are determined by the ratio of the sample size in the treatment group to the sample size in the control group times the number of matches for each case:

$$w_i = \frac{n_C}{n_T} \frac{m_{Tj}}{m_{Cj}}, \tag{4.5}$$

where w_i is the weight for each case, n_C is the number of participants in the comparison group, n_T is the number of participants in the treatment group, m_{Tj} is the number of treatment cases matched to each comparison case within each matched cluster (j), and m_{Cj} is the number of comparison cases matched to each treatment case within each matched cluster. For example, suppose that we used 1 to 3 ratio matching without replacement, which resulted in 106 cases in the treatment group and 198 cases in the comparison group. Since there are less than three times as many comparison cases as treatment cases, we know that not all treatment cases have three matches. Some ($n_T = 57$) are matched with only one comparison case, some ($n_T = 16$) are matched with two comparison cases, and some ($n_T = 26$) are matched with three comparison cases. Each treatment case will be weighted by 1, but the comparison cases will be weighted by $(198/106)(1/m_{Cj})$, where j is either 1, 2, or 3. If one treatment case is matched to one comparison case, the weight for that comparison case is 1.868; if matched to two comparison cases, the weight for each of those two comparison cases is 0.934; and if matched to three comparison cases, each comparison case is weighted by 0.623. Other statistics, such as MANOVA, chi-square test of association, logistic regression, or multinomial logistic regression, may also be used after weighting the observations in a manner like the one described above. While this is a common method of weighting, other approaches may also be used (e.g., Abadie & Imbens, 2011, 2016; Lehmann, 2006).

Within-subjects analyses account for potential correlations between outcomes. Therefore, these would be used if we could reasonably assume that the observations of the matched cases are correlated. Both (a) hierarchical linear models, in which the matched subsets are accounted for as second-level effects, and (b) generalized linear mixed models (GLMM), in which the matched subsets are random effects, may be used with either a single continuous outcome variable or a single dichotomous outcome variable.

4.2b Analyses for Other Propensity Score Methods

Analysis after subclassification. There are two common approaches to estimate the treatment effect after using PS subclassification. One is to use a two-factor analysis of variance (ANOVA), in which the experimental condition is one factor and the PS stratum is the second factor (Rosenbaum & Rubin, 1984). For example, suppose that we are comparing two groups and stratify cases into quintiles based on the propensity scores. This would give us a 2 (treatment condition) × 5 (PS stratum) design. The effects of the treatment would be tested by running a two-factor ANOVA in which both experimental condition and stratum are included in the model as main effects and as a two-way interaction. The main effect for the stratum and the interaction term serve as covariates that partial out the variance of the propensity scores (see Table 4.4). The remaining between-subjects variance (i.e., the result for the main effect for treatment) should provide an unbiased estimate for the treatment. In the example illustrated by Table 4.4, we would conclude that after accounting for propensity scores through subclassification, those in the

Table 4.4 Source Table for a Two-Way ANOVA Used to Account for Propensity Scores

Source	F	df	p
Treatment Condition	42.756	1, 190	< .001
Stratum	5.869	4, 190	< .001
Condition*Stratum	0.592	4, 190	.669

treatment group had significantly different scores from those in the control group, $F_{(1, 190)} = 42.756, p < .001$. A more common approach is to compute a between-subjects analysis, such as an independent- or dependent-samples t-test, for each stratum and either average effect estimates (i.e., t or d values) across strata (Shadish & Clark, 2002) or interpret them separately for each stratum (Han, Grogan-Kaylor, Delva, & Xie, 2014). If the dependent variable is categorical, chi-square tests or multiway frequency analyses may be used instead. If the dependent variable is count data, a Poisson or negative binomial regression may be used. This approach is similar to the previous one, in that it is based on a factorial ANOVA, except that here, we just look at the simple main effects rather than treating the stratum terms as covariates. Following the 2 × 5 design above, we would run five independent-samples t-tests, one for each stratum (see Table 4.5). This approach is more appropriate than the factorial ANOVA if the effects are very different depending on the stratum. In the example in Table 4.5, all of the mean differences are between 3.1 and 5.3, suggesting that the treatment group consistently had higher scores than the control group regardless of the probability of selecting the treatment group. Therefore, either approach may be suitable. However, if one of the strata had a negative effect, the second approach is more accurate.

Propensity score weighting. Some researchers suggest that once observations are weighted, one can simply run an independent t-test or simple regression to test the adjusted treatment effect (Holmes, 2014). However, others have found that weighting observations tends to overinflate standard errors, which results in underestimation of the treatment effect (Clark, 2015; Heckman et al., 1998). This can be controlled by using normalized or stabilized weights to reduce overweighting observations (Austin & Stuart, 2015; Hirano & Imbens, 2001; Robins, Hernán, & Brumback, 2000) and by

Table 4.5 Series of Independent t-Tests Used to Account for Propensity Scores

Stratum	M Difference	t	df	p
1	5.234	5.288	49	< .001
2	3.068	2.760	50	.008
3	4.791	4.052	42	< .001
4	4.250	2.635	26	.014
5	3.400	1.555	23	.134

bootstrapping samples to estimate standard errors (Reynolds & DesJardins, 2009; Shadish et al., 2008). As described in Chapter 3, the normalization and stabilization adjustments are simply modifications to the weights themselves, rather than the treatment effect analysis. However, using these weighting approaches may decrease the likelihood that cases with very large (e.g., .95) or small (e.g., .05) propensity scores will be overweighted and that standard errors will be inflated. If these are controlled, a traditional t-test could be used. Otherwise, standard errors may be estimated by bootstrapping the standard error of the weighted mean differences (i.e., the ATE or ATT). A t-test for the treatment effect can be computed by dividing the weighted mean differences by the average standard error of the bootstrapped sample (t = ATE/SE). Leite (2017) provides a more detailed explanation of how these standard errors can be generated and applied.

Covariate adjustment. The procedures for using covariate adjustments with propensity scores are easier than the other methods, since most computer programs estimate both multiple regressions and ANCOVAs. When using a multiple regression, you simply include the propensity score in the model as an additional predictor variable (see Equation 4.6):

$$\hat{Y} = a + b_1 X_i + b_2 e_{xi}, \qquad (4.6)$$

where $\hat{Y}$ is the predicted dependent variable, a is the constant, b_1 is the regression coefficient for the treatment, X_i is the treatment condition for each participant (0 = control and 1 = treatment), and b_2 is the regression coefficient for the propensity score. When using an ANCOVA, the treatment condition is the fixed factor and the propensity score is the covariate. The treatment effect is then based on the adjusted means and standard errors, rather than the original group means and standard deviations.

4.2c Doubly Robust Procedures

Schafer and Kang (2008) found that propensity scores may not sufficiently reduce selection bias if they are not modeled correctly. Model misspecification may occur if the PS model does not include all influential covariates that contribute to selection bias (i.e., nonignorable observations); there are several missing values on the covariates used in the model; or the functional form of the covariates is misspecified (i.e., covariates may need to be modeled using higher order terms, such as nonlinear trends or interactions). While one solution is to add interactions or higher order terms to the PS model, Schafer and Kang suggest using a doubly robust procedure, in which both the individual covariates and the propensity scores are included in the model. While Shadish et al. (2008) did not specifically test for model misspecification, they found that the doubly robust procedures often reduced more bias than when they used the PS methods alone. Doubly robust procedures can be used with any of the adjustment methods described above. The analytic procedures usually require simply using an ANCOVA with the other procedures. For example, a doubly robust matching procedure could be used to estimate a treatment effect with a two-way ANCOVA after the cases were matched on propensity scores. In this case, one could use a paired matching procedure to select the cases to be used in the analysis. Then, the matched samples would be compared in an ANCOVA that accounts for all of the covariates used to create the propensity scores. Likewise, treatment effects for subclassification and weighting would use an ANCOVA that includes individual covariates as well as either stratifying or weighting by the propensity scores. Covariate adjustments with propensity scores would include both the propensity scores and the individual covariates as covariates in an ANCOVA or regression.

4.3 Sensitivity Analysis

When applying PS methods to observational data, we assume that all the influential covariates are measured and included in the PS estimation model. However, in reality, this rarely occurs outside of laboratory or simulation studies. Hidden bias often exists when unobserved covariates cannot be included in the PS model. Sensitivity analysis of the estimated treatment effect is a procedure used to test how robust the treatment effect estimation is despite hidden bias after implementing PS methods, and how biased the treatment effect estimation may be when hidden bias exists. Unfortunately, many existing publications prior to 2018 seem to ignore sensitivity analysis, partially because of the limited availability of these procedures in most software packages. However, it is essential to assess the sensitivity of the estimated treatment effect to potential hidden bias so that we may know (a) how well a PS method reduced selection bias and (b) if the treatment effects are reliable (Rubin, 1997).

Many studies describe various methods for testing the robustness of a treatment effect that has been adjusted with propensity scores. Some of these methods include (a) a full likelihood function for unmeasured covariates with a binary outcome (Rosenbaum & Rubin, 1983); (b) Rosenbaum's (2002) bounds using a logistic model based on the randomization framework; (c) linear programming methods for upper and lower bounds with a binary outcome (Kuroki & Cai, 2008); (d) a feasible, region-based approach using inverse probability weighting (Shen, Li, Li, & Were, 2011);

and (e) PS-based sensitivity (Li, Shen, Wu, & Li, 2011). Among these methods, Rosenbaum's (2002) bounds strategy is the most frequently used technique because it is available in some statistical packages, such as R.

Rosenbaum's bound. Based on the principle of randomization inference, Rosenbaum (2002) developed a sensitivity analysis that uses a bound to assess the magnitude of the increase in uncertainty of the treatment effect estimation when hidden bias exists (Keele, 2010). The basic concept of Rosenbaum's bound is to use Γ, the log of the coefficient for the unobserved covariate, as a measure of the bias of the treatment effect (that is, the degree of departure from a randomized experiment). Rosenbaum's approach focuses on the statistical significance of the association between the outcome and the treatment conditions (Gastwirth, Krieger, & Rosenbaum, 1998; Liu, Kuramoto, & Stuart, 2013). Rosenbaum's sensitivity approaches include primal sensitivity analysis; simultaneous sensitivity analysis; and dual sensitivity analysis, which is similar to primary sensitivity analysis. In a primal sensitivity analysis, the odds ratio of the relationship between receiving the treatment and the unobserved confounder is bounded between $1/\Gamma$ and Γ, where $\Gamma < 2$. As Γ increases, so does the likelihood that the treatment estimation may change because of the hidden bias. Inferential statistics (based on p values) are often used to test the effect that Γ has on the treatment effect. For example, in Rosenbaum's sensitivity test that uses Wilcoxon's Signed Rank statistic, the model for the treatment effect is considered sensitive to hidden bias if the conclusion from an inferential test of the treatment effect changes when $\Gamma < 2$. That is, if the treatment effect estimate was significant after applying PS methods, but the upper and lower bound p values for Γ become nonsignificant (e.g., $.02 < p < .08$ using $\alpha = .05$) while $\Gamma < 2$, then the effect estimate may become biased. Likewise, if the treatment effect estimate was not significant after applying PS methods, but the upper and lower bound p values for Γ become significant (e.g., $p < .05$ for upper bound) while $\Gamma < 2$, then the effect estimate may become biased. That is, the estimated treatment effect is sensitive to the true (bias-free/bias-adjusted) odds ratio of the treatment on the outcome, even after the treatment effect was adjusted for the observed confounders. The specific randomization test used to detect this sensitivity depends on the measurement scale of the outcome variable (e.g., binary, continuous, or ordinal). However, a different function for sensitivity analysis is available for multiple group comparisons.

Simultaneous sensitivity analysis. This approach allows a researcher to test the effects of the sensitivity of the treatment effect to the relationship that the unobserved covariate has on both the treatment condition and the outcome. This approach uses (a) an upper bound (Γ) for the odds ratio of the relationship between the treatment condition and the unobserved covariate, and (b) an upper bound (Δ) for the odds ratio of the relationship between the outcome and the unobserved covariate. The point is to find the threshold in which the combinations of Γ and Δ are nonsignificant, indicating that the estimation of the treatment effect is sensitive to the unobserved covariate. Liu et al. (2013) provided an applied example in which the effect of the independent variable (exposure to mother's death) became sensitive to the unobserved covariate ($p = .08$) when $\Gamma = 7.39$ and $\Delta = 1.84$. That is, a maternal death by suicide was no longer significantly related to an offspring's hospitalization for suicide attempt when $\Gamma = 7.39$ and $\Delta = 1.84$, suggesting a moderate sensitivity to the unobserved covariate.

4.4 Summary of the Chapter

PS methods are meant to allow researchers to make adjustments to the sample or statistical analysis that correct selection bias when estimating the treatment effect. For propensity scores to be effective, (a) covariates must be balanced after applying the PS method (e.g., after matching or weighting on them) and (b) researchers must use an appropriate analysis based on the particular PS method used. Covariate balance is most often assessed by the mean difference of the covariate between groups (selection bias) or the standardized difference of the group means of the covariate (standardized bias). Both of these should be relatively small (e.g., $SB < 5\%$). The checklist at the end of this chapter is provided to help you determine whether or not propensity scores have sufficiently balanced the covariates after the PS procedure.

When using a greedy (e.g., paired) type of PS matching, basic inferential statistics, such as *t*-tests, may be used to estimate treatment effects from the matched sample, assuming that all covariates are balanced in the matched data. However, if ratio matching or sampling with replacement is used, cases need to be weighted by the ratio of matched cases first. For subclassification, strata are included in the two-group comparison either by running a two-factor (group × strata) ANOVA or by comparing group means (with a *t*-test or one-way ANOVA) for each stratum. Analysis for weighting on propensity scores is similar to that for complex matching procedures, except that weights are based on the propensity scores rather than the ratio of the matches. When using covariate adjustments with propensity scores, we can include the propensity scores as a covariate in either an ANCOVA or a multiple regression. Finally, to ensure that the treatment effect estimate is robust against potential hidden bias, a sensitivity analysis should be conducted as the last step.

4.5 An Example

Using the Playworks data that we described in Chapter 2.4, we will demonstrate how to (a) evaluate the balance of covariates before and after PS matching, (b) test the treatment effect after PS matching, and (c) conduct a sensitivity analysis. The basic codes for these analyses and more detailed descriptions for these procedures, outputs, and interpretations are provided on the book's website. We only demonstrate what results can be expected from some sample analyses and how to interpret them in this text.

4.5a Example for Checking the Balance of Covariates Before and After Propensity Score Matching

Statistical check. After running PS matching procedures using nearest neighbor matching in Section 3.4, a new matched data file was created. Many statistical packages provide a variety of balance statistics described in Section 4.1 that will allow you to check whether or not the covariates are balanced in the matched data (e.g., mean differences, standard bias reduction, or percentage bias reduction). Table 4.6 presents the balance results for our example after using nearest neighbor, paired matching (1:1) without replacement.

You can see that, before matching, the mean difference of the propensity score is 0.102 with a standardized bias of 75.03%, indicating that the average of the propensity scores in each group was very different. After matching, the mean difference of the propensity scores is reduced to 0.006 with a standardized bias of 4.45%, which indicates a significant bias reduction. Furthermore, since *SB* is less than 5%, it meets the most conservative standard for balance as recommended by Caliendo and Kopeinig (2008). The percentage of bias reduction is 93.66%, which also indicates a sufficient amount of overall bias reduction, meaning that the bias reduced among all 16 covariates is substantial. It is worth noting that, even though the overall bias reduction is sufficient, in some procedures, PS matching may increase bias for those covariates that may have been balanced prior to matching. It is not unusual for matching to overcorrect or worsen bias in matched samples for these variables because matching is based on the propensity score, which is an aggregate of all the covariates, not individual ones. In our example in Chapter 2, we pointed out that one covariate, relationships with other students (S_CONFLICTRES_RELATIONSHIPS), had a weak relationship with the treatment variable; therefore, it was already balanced. In Table 4.6, you can see that this covariate (highlighted in bold) had a mean difference of −0.217 and standard bias 11% before matching, but the mean difference increased to −0.252 and the standard

Table 4.6 Covariate Balance Results Before and After Nearest Neighbor Matching

	Before Matching					After Matching					
	Means Treated	Means Control	SD Control	Mean Diff	Standard Bias %	Means Treated	Means Control	SD Control	Mean Diff	Standard Bias %	% Reduction
Propensity score	0.236	0.133	0.105	0.102	75.03	0.226	0.220	0.118	0.006	4.45	93.66
s_gender	0.517	0.492	0.598	0.025	4.59	0.517	0.476	0.501	0.041	8.14	−61.33
s_grade	4.483	4.494	0.500	−0.011	−2.21	4.483	4.490	0.502	−0.007	−1.36	38.62
S_CLIMATE_COMMUNITY	3.013	2.522	1.483	0.491	45.08	3.013	3.016	0.434	−0.003	−0.70	99.39
S_CLIMATE_SCHOOLSAFETY	2.565	2.305	1.539	0.260	18.88	2.565	2.465	1.266	0.099	8.07	61.83
S_CONFLICTRES_AGGRESSIVE	1.342	1.381	1.108	−0.039	−4.59	1.342	1.345	0.459	−0.003	−0.57	93.33
S_CONFLICTRES_RELATIONSHIPS	2.744	2.960	1.567	−0.217	**−11.00**	2.744	2.995	1.870	**−0.252**	**−12.00**	**−16.21**
S_CONFLICTRES_AGGBELIEF	1.516	1.598	1.185	−0.083	−8.70	1.516	1.553	0.632	−0.037	−5.92	54.70
S_LEARNING_RECESSEFFECT	2.501	2.188	1.810	0.313	23.19	2.501	2.540	0.674	−0.039	−6.01	87.68
S_LEARNING_SPORTSEFFECT	2.533	2.207	2.101	0.326	18.96	2.533	2.633	0.897	−0.100	−9.32	69.32
S_LEARNING_ENGAGEMENT	3.255	3.100	1.143	0.155	18.00	3.255	3.242	0.476	0.013	2.82	91.84
S_RECESS_ORGANIZED	2.056	1.850	1.241	0.206	21.40	2.056	2.111	0.583	−0.055	−9.69	73.19
S_RECESS_ENJOYMENT	3.602	3.504	1.240	0.098	10.63	3.602	3.637	0.499	−0.035	−7.79	64.22
S_YOUTHDEV_INTERACTIONS	3.320	3.073	1.592	0.247	20.60	3.320	3.290	1.157	0.030	3.24	88.00
S_YOUTHDEV_PEERCONFLICT	2.220	1.890	1.469	0.330	28.51	2.220	2.338	0.791	−0.118	−15.62	64.14
S_YOUTHDEV_PEERNONCONFLICT	1.844	1.461	1.734	0.382	29.22	1.844	1.787	1.168	0.057	6.00	85.18
S_PHYSICAL_SELFCONCEPT	1.730	1.645	1.067	0.086	11.16	1.730	1.744	0.229	−0.013	−6.11	84.53

bias increased to 12% after matching. The percentage reduction of −16.21% indicates that the bias *increased* after matching. In this situation, we should consider removing this covariate from the PS model.

Graphical check. A variety of graphs can also be produced that allow researchers to evaluate how well propensity scores reduced selection bias. Jitter plots and histograms permit one to have a visual check on the global balance before and after PS matching, and Q-Q plots can be used to measure the balance for each individual covariate. To generate these graphs, you may follow the scripts provided on the book's website.

For example, both the Jitter plot (Figure 4.1) and histogram (Figure 4.2) generated as a part of the results from the nearest neighbor matching show the distributions of the propensity scores for the treatment and control groups. The Jitter plot includes PS distributions for both the matched and unmatched cases after matching. Since we matched all the treated cases in our matching procedure, Figure 4.1 shows only three distributions. From these, you can see that the data points in the matched sample distributions show a very similar pattern, while the unmatched data points pile up near the left side of the distribution. The histograms include PS distributions for the original (raw) sample prior to matching and the matched sample. Here you can see that the distributions for the matched cases are much more similar to each other than the distributions prior to matching.

4.5b Estimating the Treatment Effect After Propensity Score Matching

The analyses for the treatment effect can be estimated using a variety of procedures. Theoretically, we can use a *t*-test with the matched sample if all

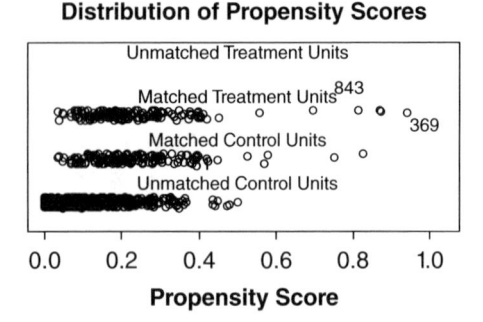

Figure 4.1 Jitter plots for the matched cases and unmatched cases.

Figure 4.2 Histograms for the raw data and the matched cases.

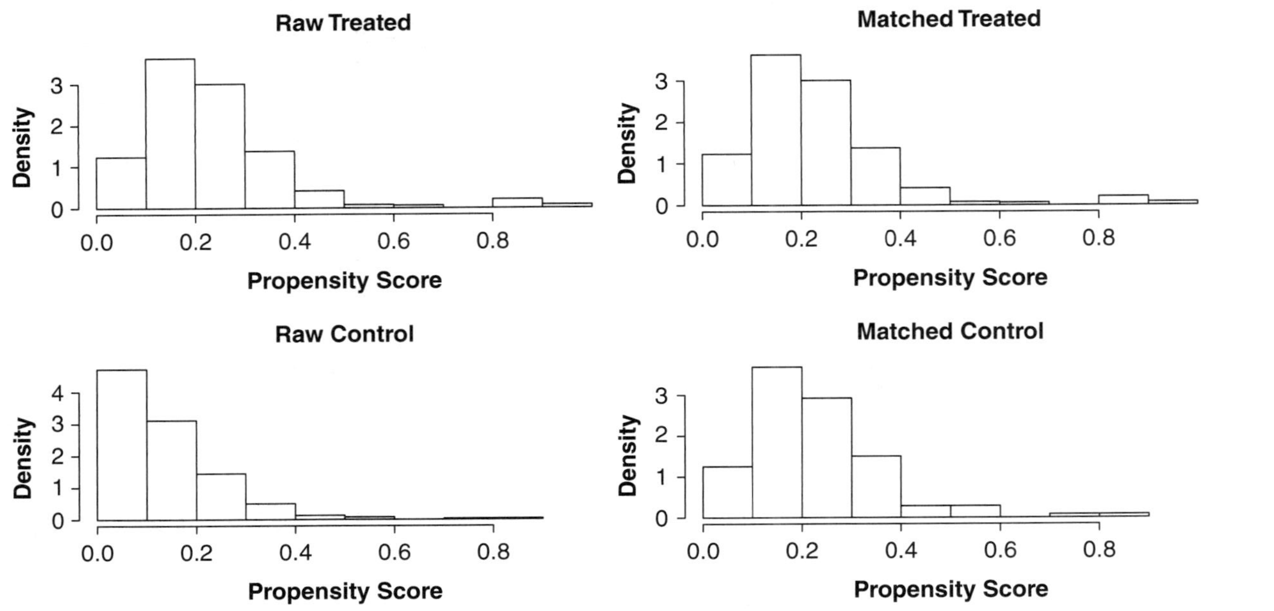

83

the covariates are well balanced after matching. If some covariates are still unbalanced after matching, we need to control them in the final treatment estimation. This is often done by including the covariates in the treatment effect model in an analysis of covariance or regression. Here, we present an example using an independent-samples t-test; however, other types of analyses are demonstrated on the book's website. The results of the treatment effect estimation from this t-test are interpreted the same way as those from an unadjusted inferential statistic.

Table 4.7 presents the results from an independent-samples t-test using the data that were obtained after the nearest neighbor matching procedure from Chapter 3. Assignment to Playworks (S_TREATMENT) is the independent variable, and students' reported feelings of safety at recess (S_CLIMATE_RECESSSAFETY) was used as the outcome variable. These results show that the treatment group has a significantly higher mean score on students' perceptions of safety at recess than the control group, $t_{(227)} = 2.306$, $p = .022$. This implies that the treatment effect is statistically significant estimated from the matched data. Although the same conclusion could be made from the t-test with the original data without matching, with $t_{(989)} = 2.306$ and $p < .001$, the effect from the matched data is not as strong, but it is presumably more accurate, since the covariates are less biased. Despite the reduction in bias on the observed covariates, this treatment effect may not be accurate if there is any hidden bias. Therefore, we should assess how sensitive this treatment effect estimation is to hidden bias.

4.5c Sensitivity Analysis

In this example, we used Rosenbaum's R-bounds to check the sensitivity of the treatment effect estimation from the matched data to hidden bias. Table 4.8 shows the results of Rosenbaum's Sensitivity Test using a Wilcoxon Signed Rank test with Rosenbaum's bounds for the p values. In Rosenbaum's test, Gamma (Γ) is the odds of differential assignment to the treatment condition due to unobserved factors. Following the common

Table 4.7 Independent Sample t-Test Results on S_CLIMATE_RECESSSAFETY

Data	Treat Mean	Control Mean	Independent t	df	p	Mean Diff	95% Lower	95% Upper	Treat	Control
NN1:1	2.896	2.622	2.306	292	0.022	0.274	0.12	0.04	147	147
Original	2.896	2.483	5.335	989	< .001	0.413	0.163	0.662	147	844

practice used in social and behavioral sciences, we set the maximum value for Γ to 2 with increments of 0.1. From the table, we can see that when $\Gamma = 1$, $p = .0113$ for the treatment effect estimation when there are no additional confounders or hidden bias. With an increase of 0.1, the p value is still significant at $\alpha = .05$, indicating that the treatment effect is still significant if the odds of one person being in the treatment group are 1.1 times higher because of different values on an unobserved covariate. However, when $\Gamma = 1.2$, the p value increases to .0861, which suggests a nonsignificant effect. This means that if the odds of a person being in the treatment group are only 1.2 times higher because of different values on an unobserved covariate, even though the other 16 covariates are balanced between the treated and control groups, the treatment effect may not be statistically significant. In other words, with only a slight increase in selection bias due to an unobserved covariate, the statistical inference would change.

The book's companion website at **study.sagepub.com/researchmethods/ qass/bai&clark** provides instructions and code for conducting a sensitivity analysis, interpretations, and annotated output for the results from Rosenbaum's sensitivity analysis.

Table 4.8 Rosenbaum Sensitivity Test for Wilcoxon Signed Rank p-value

	p-value	
Gamma	*Lower Bound*	*Upper Bound*
1.0	0.0113	0.0113
1.1	0.0028	0.0359
1.2	0.0006	0.0861
1.3	0.0001	0.1668
1.4	0.0000	0.2744
1.5	0.0000	0.3980
1.6	0.0000	0.5240
1.7	0.0000	0.6405
1.8	0.0000	0.7397
1.9	0.0000	0.8187
2.0	0.0000	0.8780

Note: Unconfounded estimate is 0.0113.

Checklist for Testing Covariate Balance

☑ Compute the standardized bias estimate using Equation 4.2 for each continuous (ratio or interval) covariate used in your PS model. Is this less than 10%?
- If so, that covariate is assumed to be well balanced.
- If not, check the PS estimation model and any unmeasured covariates.

☑ Compute the standardized bias estimate using Equation 4.3 for each categorical (nominal or ordinal) covariate used in your PS model. Is this less than 10%?
- If so, that covariate is assumed to be well balanced.
- If not, check the PS estimation model and any unmeasured covariates.

☑ Compute the percent of bias reduction using Equation 4.4 for each covariate. Is this more than 80%?
- If a covariate is balanced and bias was reduced by 80% or more, the PS method significantly reduced the selection bias of the covariate.
- If a covariate is balanced and bias was not reduced by 80% or more, the covariate may have been sufficiently balanced before the PS adjustment.
- If a covariate is not balanced and bias was reduced by 80% or more, use a doubly robust model when estimating the treatment effects by including the covariate in the statistical model.
- If a covariate is not balanced and bias was not reduced by 80% or more, the PS adjustment did not sufficiently reduce bias. Try using another adjustment method or including higher order trends in your PS model.

Study Questions for Chapter 4

1. Using the *First Year Seminar* dataset (located at **study.sagepub.com/researchmethods/qass/bai&clark**) compute the (a) selection bias and (b) standardized bias for each of the 10 covariates before any statistical adjustment.

2. Compute propensity scores using all 10 covariates in the *First Year Seminar* dataset, and match students who participated in the first year seminar (*Univ101* = 1) to those who did not (*Univ101* = 0) using paired (1 to 1) matching without replacement. (This is the same exercise from

Chapter 2, Problem 4). Using the matched sample, compute the following for each covariate:

a. Selection bias
b. Standardized bias
c. Percent bias reduction (use the estimates from Problem 1 as the bias before matching)
d. Are any of the covariates in the matched sample still unbalanced (i.e., $d > .1$ or $SB = 10$)?
e. Are there any covariates for which there was less than an 80% reduction in bias?

3. Using the matched sample that you generated in Problem 2, estimate the treatment effect of the first year seminar program on the following:

   a. First-year grade point average (FirstYrGPA) using an independent-samples t-test
   b. Second-year retention (EnrollYr2) using a chi-square test of association

4. Using the original *First Year Seminar* dataset (before matching), estimate the treatment effect of the first year seminar program on the following:

   a. First-year grade point average (FirstYrGPA) using an independent-samples t-test. How does this result compare with the one you ran on the matched sample?
   b. Second-year retention (EnrollYr2) using a chi-square test of association. How does this result compare with the one you ran on the matched sample?

5. Using the results from Problem 4, run a sensitivity analysis and determine the following:

   a. What does it mean when the p value for Γ is above the .05 threshold?
   b. How much increase in Γ is necessary before the treatment effect estimation becomes sensitive to hidden bias?

CHAPTER 5. CONCLUSION

The final chapter discusses the limitations and restrictions in using PS methods, provides suggestions to address limitations, summarizes the most important points that have been presented in the previous chapters, and remarks on the development of PS methods. While many researchers have found PS methods very effective in reducing selection bias in causal studies without random assignment, some have not. Therefore, we will discuss conditions under which PS methods may not yield unbiased results. This chapter discusses alternatives or suggestions to minimize the limitations of PS methods.

5.1 Limitations of the Propensity Score Methods and How to Address Them

As researchers embrace the advantages in using PS methods, it is essential that they also understand the limitations of these methods. Researchers are responsible for providing sufficient empirical evidence that they controlled for potential limitations, addressed unsolved issues, and appropriately interpreted their research findings after implementing PS methods (Pan & Bai, 2016). While the PS methods are intended to reduce selection bias and improve internal validity in observational studies, it is possible that bias can be increased if propensity scores are not used properly.

5.1a Hidden Bias

Failing to meet the assumption of ignorability (or the Ignorable Treatment Assignment assumption) may prevent researchers from obtaining an unbiased treatment effect estimation even after using PS methods. In theory, assignment to treatment conditions will be unrelated to any variable other than the outcome after accounting for a set of observed covariates. Therefore, this assumption requires that all of the confounding variables be measured and properly modeled when estimating the propensity scores. Propensity scores can only be estimated using the observed covariates, but there could be other, unknown confounders that influence the treatment effect. Therefore, in practice, this assumption may not be met, as hidden bias usually exists when *unobserved* covariates are omitted from the PS model (Joffe & Rosenbaum, 1999; Rosenbaum & Rubin, 1983; Rubin, 1997). Therefore, the accuracy of the PS estimates and their ability to sufficiently reduce selection bias in treatment effects could be seriously affected by these missing predictors or confounders (Greenland, 1989; Hosmer & Lemeshow, 2000; Rothman, Greenland, & Lash, 1998; Weitzen, Lapane, Toledano, Hume, & Mor, 2004). While we may not be able to account for all sources of hidden bias, as some cannot be easily measured or obtained, we can limit the sources of hidden bias through careful design planning. This is best done by deliberate and thorough selection of covariates, which is guided by theory. Ideally, we should include all unbalanced, influential covariates that can be measured in the PS estimation model (Pan & Bai, 2016). Knowing the likelihood that hidden bias may exist, it is also important to conduct a sensitivity analysis to test how robust our final treatment model is to hidden bias from potential unobserved covariates (Pan & Bai, 2016; Rosenbaum & Rubin, 1983). If the results of the sensitivity analysis indicate that omitting a covariate will likely alter the treatment effect, researchers should carefully interpret how sensitive the treatment effect estimate is to the existence of hidden bias (Li et al., 2011).

5.1b Issues With Propensity Score Matching

PS matching is perhaps the most popular of the PS methods and has gained considerable notoriety for its ability to create samples that may replicate those from randomized designs (Rosenbaum & Rubin, 1985). However, it has received a lot of criticism over the past few years (e.g., King & Nielsen, 2016; Pearl, 2010). First, if hidden bias exists, matching on the propensity scores will not create comparable groups because the propensity scores are not modeled correctly. Second, PS matching requires sufficient overlap or common support of the propensity scores. If the common support is not sufficient, the matched data will not represent the original sample, as matching often drops cases that are dissimilar. Therefore, it is very likely that PS matching will drop cases with very high or low propensity scores, which means that we may not be able to generalize the treatment effects using the matched data to the populations that the original sample represents. A third problem with PS matching is that researchers often struggle to find the most appropriate matching method for their study. As we have discussed previously, there are many options when matching on propensity scores, and researchers have found that the best method often depends on the specific conditions of their data or the way that propensity scores are estimated (Harder et al., 2010; Lee et al., 2010; Pan & Bai, 2015a; Stone & Tang, 2013). For example, the amount of bias reduced is significantly different depending on whether matches are made with or without replacement (Pan & Bai, 2015a); this effect is particularly pronounced when sample sizes are small. Bias reduction may also be affected by the number of control cases that are matched with each treatment case. If we have proportionately more control cases than treated cases (or vice versa), ratio matching (1:m or m:1) might be beneficial. This type of matching will enable us to use more information from the original sample to represent a target population, which will increase the external validity or generalizability of the outcome estimation.

Despite these criticisms, in theory, PS matching is still a good approach for improving the validity of causal inferences in observational studies. The key concern is not with the method itself, but if it is used appropriately. First, researchers should fully understand the assumptions of using PS methods. Second, it is critical to select appropriate matching procedures based on the specific characteristics of the data. Third, it is essential to check for covariate balance after matching on propensity scores. If there are still some covariates left unbalanced after PS matching, these covariates should be controlled in the treatment effect estimation model. Finally, sensitivity analysis must be used to address how robust the causal effect estimation with propensity scores is to unobserved covariates after matching on propensity scores.

5.1c Sample Reduction or Exclusion

As a function of matching, only the matched pairs will be retained for analyses, and the unmatched cases are excluded. However, excluding a large proportion of cases significantly reduces the sample size. When a large proportion of cases is excluded, it poses two potential problems: (a) The new matched dataset may no longer represent its target population, and (b) this may reduce the statistical power when estimating the treatment effect (Bai, 2011; Weitzen et al., 2004). This situation is most likely to occur when there is insufficient common support between the treatment and comparison groups, in which case researchers should not use PS matching.

One way to reduce a lack of common support is to use large samples (Rubin, 1997). Not only do large datasets increase the common support between groups; they also produce more stable results than those with small sample sizes (Bai, 2011; Hirano, Imbens, & Ridder, 2003; Månsson, Joffe, Sun, & Hennessy, 2007; Rubin, 1997). Although Rosenbaum and Rubin (1983) have argued that PS methods can sufficiently remove bias in observational studies with either large or small sample sizes, others (Bai, 2011; Rubin, 1997) have found that larger datasets (e.g., national data) provide more stable results when using PS methods to make causal inferences. A second way to limit the number of cases dropped when matching is to use *complex* matching methods. For example, optimal matching, full matching, and matching with replacement will often select more matches than caliper matching or matching without replacement. Therefore, they are better options when working with small sample sizes.

5.1d Issues With Propensity Score Weighting

PS weighting has some advantages over PS matching in its capacity to handle complex data (e.g., nested or longitudinal) and limit sample size reduction. However, PS weighting is still susceptible to hidden bias and is likely to overweight cases. For example, when using an inverse probability of treatment weighting (IPTW) procedure, treated cases with small propensity scores and control cases with large propensity scores may be assigned very large weights. Such weights can increase the variability and the standard errors of the estimated treatment effect (Austin & Stuart, 2015), which reduce statistical power. PS weighting is also sensitive to model misspecification when estimating propensity scores (Freedman & Berk, 2008), which can produce a negative effect and therefore increase the bias when estimating treatment effects (Harder et al., 2010; Olmos & Govindasamy, 2015; Stone & Tang, 2013).

To address the above issues, other types of weighting methods should be considered. These methods include stabilized weights to use the marginal probability of treatment and control cases in the overall sample (Lee, Lessler, & Stuart, 2011) and the trimmed or truncated weights by setting up a threshold using quantiles of the distributions of the weights (Cole & Hernán, 2008) to avoid overweighting issues (Austin & Stuart, 2015). Regarding the model misspecification issues, researchers should verify the model fit to effectively use PS weighting.

5.2 Summary of Propensity Score Procedures

5.2a Covariate Selection

The primary goal of PS methods is to fix an imperfect design so that we can make strong causal conclusions. PS methods are often used with existing observational data; however, it is also beneficial to use them when it is not possible to randomly assign participants into research conditions. Researchers should determine on which covariates to collect data a priori so that PS methods are most effective in reducing selection bias. Therefore, it still requires substantial planning of the design from the beginning of the study. In such cases, it is necessary to consider the covariates that will most likely affect both selection into conditions and how they relate to your outcome variables. The best approach for determining this is to conduct a thorough literature review and consult experts. This will allow researchers to collect data on these specific variables and increase the likelihood that they have accounted for all sources of nonignorable bias. Unfortunately, researchers often find themselves in situations where they have to salvage a study with a poor design, for which the data have already been collected. This poses a considerable problem: They may not have the data to create good propensity scores. In such cases, you may still estimate and apply PS methods, but be aware that PS methods may not sufficiently reduce selection bias.

In sum, the best propensity scores are estimated based on covariates that (a) are related to both the treatment conditions and outcomes, (b) are measured prior to treatment, and (c) account for all sources of bias. While it is unlikely that we will be able to account for *all* sources of selection bias, we can increase the probability that we will account for most sources of bias by choosing what covariates are measured prior to any data collection.

Using the variables that we have available to us, we can statistically examine which ones are related to treatment conditions and the outcome variables. In two-group designs (i.e., comparing one treatment and one control group), we may compute the standardized bias using Equations 4.2 and 4.3. Any covariate that has more than a small (i.e., $SB > 10\%$ or $d > .1$) or trivial (i.e., $SB > 5\%$ or $d > .05$) amount of bias is worth considering for inclusion in the PS model. While other inferential statistics may be used to assess how the covariates are related to treatment conditions, using effect sizes or measures of standardized bias are less likely to be influenced by large or small sample sizes. Similarly, the relationship between each covariate and the outcome variable can be assessed with effect sizes. Pearson or Spearman correlations may be used for continuous covariates and continuous outcomes; standardized mean differences may be used for dichotomous covariates and continuous outcomes; and odds ratios may be used for either continuous or categorical covariates and dichotomous outcomes. Again, any covariate that has more than a small or trivial relationship with the outcome variable is worth considering for the model.

If covariates are related to both treatment condition and outcome, be sure to include them in the PS model. Although covariates that are related to only the outcome variable will have a limited effect on covariate balance, they may still affect the treatment effect. Therefore, these should also be included in the model. If covariates are related to the treatment condition, but not the outcome variable, researchers must consider the temporal precedence. Remember that propensity scores are used to measure how certain characteristics influence self-selection into conditions. This requires that the covariates existed prior to treatment assignment. If a covariate is measured after the treatment, it is not a preexisting characteristic and may be affected by the treatment. Therefore, include covariates that are related to the treatment condition if they were measured (or existed) before the treatment.

5.2b Estimating the Propensity Scores

Although there are several options for computing propensity scores, the two most common approaches are logistic regression and tree-based ensemble methods. Both methods permit the inclusion of several categorical and continuous covariates and weight the propensity scores by the relative relationship that the covariates have with the treatment condition. That is, covariates that are strongly related to treatment conditions are given more weight in the propensity model than those with weak relationships. Logistic regression is fairly straightforward, as it uses similar modeling methods as ordinary least squares regression, and it is available in most statistical packages. Tree-based ensemble methods are more stable (and more generalizable), as they aggregate not only the covariates, but several PS models as well. While some researchers have preferences for one method over the other—and have found small differences in the estimation methods—either approach creates good propensity scores as long as all nonignorable covariates are included in the models.

With either approach, the resulting propensity scores are the predicted probabilities of being in a treatment condition, and most statistical packages will automatically provide these values (often labeled as unstandardized predicted probabilities). A participant with a propensity score that is close to one will likely be in the treatment group, while someone with a propensity score close to zero will most likely be in the comparison group. In the event that PS distributions are not normal, propensity scores can be transformed using a logit transformation to reduce skewness.

5.2c Common Support of the Propensity Score

Prior to using the propensity scores in an adjustment, it is essential to assess the common support of the propensity scores. This may be examined using graphs, effect sizes, or inferential tests to compare group differences on the propensity scores. Simply comparing a histogram of the propensity scores for each group allows the researcher to see how well the PS distributions overlap. The greater the overlap or the common support, the more comparable the groups will be after the PS adjustment. The mean differences and standardized mean differences of the propensity scores provide quantitative values for the amount of overlap. These differences should be very small. While there is no clear criterion for an acceptable difference between the group means, Rubin (2001) recommends that the *standardized* mean difference is less than .5. Other researchers (Bai, 2015) recommend that a certain proportion (e.g., 75%) of propensity scores in the treatment group overlap with the range of propensity scores in the comparison group. The difference between the distributions of the propensity scores can also be assessed using inferential (or significance) tests, such as an independent-samples Kolmogorov-Smirnov test. However, be aware that these hypothesis tests are influenced by very small or large sample sizes and may not be appropriate for propensity scores, since our goal is not to generalize the PS distributions to a population. If the PS distributions are similar to each other, the sufficient common support assumption is met. However, if the assumption is violated, each of the adjustment methods will be problematic in its own way. Greedy matching will make several poor matches, and caliper matching will drop several cases. Subclassification will have unequal cell sizes in the highest and lowest strata, while PS weighting may overweight cases with exceptionally high or low propensity scores, and covariate adjustment may suffer from a restricted range of the covariate in one or both groups.

5.2d Summary of the Adjustment Methods

After propensity scores are obtained, they can be used in different ways to adjust for selection bias. The four most commonly used PS adjustment methods are matching, subclassification, weighting, and covariate adjustment.

Propensity score matching. Matching identifies and pairs or groups similar cases from experimental and control groups based on the proximity of their propensity scores. The most practical matching typologies include nearest neighbor matching, caliper matching, optimal matching, and full matching. While all matching methods typically reduce bias, caliper matching and optimal matching have consistently reduced the most bias. In addition to varying the matching typology, other approaches may be applied with PS matching, such as matching with replacement or having more participants in the control group than in the treatment group. Both of these approaches increase the likelihood that all treatment cases will be well matched to a control case.

Subclassification. Subclassification classifies all of the participants into several categories or strata based on their propensity scores so that each stratum includes participants from the treatment and control groups. Although subclassification usually permits the inclusion of all cases, some cells may contain few or no units. Reducing the number of strata or changing the cut-points that classify participants into a specific stratum may reduce this problem. Cut-points may be defined by percentile intervals (e.g., 20% of the cases in each stratum) or PS intervals (e.g., the range of the propensity scores in each stratum is .2).

Propensity score weighting. Weighting attempts to balance treatment and control groups by multiplying observations by a weight based on the propensity score. Two commonly used PS weighting estimators are used to find (a) the average treatment effect (ATE) by weighting observations in both the treatment and control groups by the inverse of the propensity score, or (b) the average treatment effect for the treated (ATT) by weighting just the observations in the comparison group by the odds of the propensity score. While PS weighting has become more popular in recent years, it is important to be aware that it can be particularly sensitive to outliers and model misspecification.

Covariate adjustment. Propensity scores can be used as a covariate in an ANCOVA or a multiple regression to reduce the confounding effect from a set of covariates on the outcome estimations by accounting for the correlation between the propensity scores and the dependent variable. Although many studies have found that this is an effective method for removing bias, other researchers have suggested that it is not robust against violations of statistical assumptions for ANCOVAs. In cases when covariate adjustment with propensity scores alone is not sufficient, using doubly robust models, which include individual predictors in addition to propensity scores, may reduce additional selection bias.

5.2e Checking Covariate and Propensity Score Balance

Once statistical adjustments are made to the observations, it is important to assess how well the PS methods balanced the individual covariates between the treatment and control groups. While researchers may use hypothesis tests, such as a *t*-test, to examine the balance of continuous covariates or a chi-square to test the balance for categorical covariates, results from these tests should be supported by other tests of balance. It is generally preferred to use standardized bias (*SB*) estimates and percent of bias reduction (*PBR*) to determine how well PS methods reduce selection bias.

5.2f Estimating the Treatment Effects

If PS matching was used so that each treatment case was matched to one control case, adjusted treatment effects can be made using a traditional univariate or multivariate test. For most studies, we recommend using a between-subjects analysis to estimate the treatment effects (i.e., independent-samples t-test or chi-square test of association for one outcome variable; Hotelling's T for more than one outcome variable). A within-subjects analysis may be used (i.e., paired-samples t-test or a McNemar's test for one outcome variable; repeated measures Hotelling's T for more than one outcome variable) if the treatment and comparison cases are substantially well matched. If complex matching was used, observations must be weighted before using a between-subjects univariate or multivariate test. Hierarchical linear models or generalized linear mixed models that account for matched subsets can be used as within-subjects analyses (see Table 5.1).

There are two common approaches to estimating the treatment effect when using PS subclassification. One is to use a two-factor analysis of variance (ANOVA) in which the experimental condition is one factor and the PS strata are the second factor (Rosenbaum & Rubin, 1984). The other approach is to compute a between-subjects analysis, such as an independent-samples t-test, for each stratum. If the dependent variable is categorical, chi-square or multiway frequency analyses may be used instead. If the dependent variable is count data, a Poisson or negative binomial regression may be used.

Table 5.1 Tests Used With Paired Matching

	Dependent Variable	*Univariate*	*Multivariate*
Between-Subjects	Continuous	• Independent-samples t-test • One-way analysis of variance (ANOVA) • Ordinary least squares regression	• Hotelling's T • Wilks's lambda
	Categorical	• Chi-square test of association • Multinomial logistic regression • Logistic regression	
Within-Subjects	Continuous	• Paired-samples t-test repeated measures ANOVA • Regression adjustment used with difference scores	• Repeated measures Hotelling's T • Repeated measures Wilks's lambda
	Categorical	• McNemar's test	

As with complex matching, once observations are weighted, traditional between-subjects analyses (like those listed in Table 5.1) may be run, but only if there are no extremely high or low propensity scores. If there are extreme propensity scores, overweighting can be controlled by using normalized or stabilized weights and by estimating standard errors from bootstrapped samples. Covariate adjustments with propensity scores simply require that you include the propensity scores as a covariate in an ANCOVA or in a multiple regression.

5.2g Sensitivity Analysis

The assumption of ignorability (or Ignorable Treatment Assignment) is perhaps the most commonly violated assumption when using PS methods. This occurs when researchers fail to include all covariates that contribute to the selection bias. This may occur for many reasons: Researchers may overlook covariates that contribute to bias when collecting data (e.g., not able to identify confounding variables); there are data collection constraints (e.g., not able to obtain sensitive information); it is infeasible to measure these covariates; or secondary data do not include the covariates. In any event, we must consider that the validity of our study may be affected by this hidden bias. Therefore, sensitivity analysis should be used to determine the reliability of our treatment effect and how robust it is despite potential hidden biases. While there are many methods for conducting a sensitivity analysis, Rosenbaum's (2002) approach is used most often.

The procedure consists of setting bounds, which are an interval of acceptable treatment estimates, from a logistic model based on the randomization framework. The researcher varies the *possible* odds of receiving the treatment by introducing a series of hypothetical (i.e., simulated) covariates to see how much these odds affect the treatment effects. At this point, the treatment effects have already been adjusted with PS methods, so we are examining the necessity of including the hypothetical covariates in the PS model.

Ideally, the covariates should be variables that would likely influence treatment assignment and the outcome, but were not included in the analysis, and vary in their levels of selection bias (i.e., moderately to strongly correlated to the treatment conditions and/or the outcome). The theoretical covariates represent the hidden bias that may exist in a study. If the inclusion of the theoretical covariates falls within the bounds, one may reasonably conclude that the covariates do not impact the study significantly to change the conclusion from the estimated treatment effects.

5.3 Final Comments

5.3a Are Propensity Score Methods Worth the Trouble?

As with any good evaluation of an intervention, evaluating the utility of a methodological approach also requires a cost-benefit analysis. Clearly, many researchers believe that PS methods are worth the time and effort required to conduct the procedures that we have described in this book. However, researchers should also understand the limitations of and concerns with using PS methods. In this section, we will summarize the arguments for and against using PS methods to reduce selection bias.

Those who favor the use of PS methods make the following points:

- When used properly, they effectively reduce bias. There are a number of methodological studies that consistently demonstrate that PS methods can reduce selection bias in nonrandomized comparisons regardless of the specific approach (Austin & Schuster, 2016; Bai, 2011; Dehejia & Wahba, 2002; Harder et al., 2010; Shadish et al., 2008; Stone & Tang, 2013).

- They are often more effective in reducing bias than other statistical adjustments, such as traditional covariate adjustment or matching methods (Grunwald & Mayhew, 2008; Stürmer et al., 2006). This is likely explained by the difference in the models. Traditional covariate adjustments, such as ANCOVA and multiple regressions, may reduce the effects of the covariates, but these procedures do not necessarily improve the balance between treatment groups. Propensity scores are modeled based on how well the covariates predict treatment assignment, not the outcome. Therefore, the groups are more likely to be equivalent. Traditional matching and subclassification, which use individual covariates, are also problematic in that it is often difficult to find exact matches for continuous variables, especially when matching on multiple covariates.

Critics of PS methods point out the following:

- Propensity scores require more time and effort than other approaches that work just as well. Although several studies in a meta-analysis by Stürmer et al. (2006) found that propensity scores reduced more selection bias than traditional covariate adjustment, many studies found no difference between the two approaches. However, it should be pointed out that they also noted that many of the PS studies may not have been conducted appropriately. Schafer and Kang (2008) suggest that many of the traditional adjustment methods may also be misspecified. That is, both covariates and interactions between covariates and treatment conditions should be used when adjusting for selection bias. However, even this may not completely eliminate selection bias.

- There are other methods, such as selection models and cluster-based methods, that reduce bias just as well as PS methods (D'Attoma, Camillo, & Clark, 2017; Heckman & Navarro-Lozano, 2004).

Others recommend that PS methods may be used, but not under certain conditions:

- While PS matching is one of the most common applications for propensity scores, it has recently been criticized as being inappropriate. Contrary to its intended purpose, some researchers (King & Nielsen, 2016; Pearl, 2010) claim that PS matching may actually increase covariate imbalance and treatment bias. While King and Nielsen suggest that this is less likely to occur in other PS methods and still advocate other forms of matching, they recommend that researchers avoid matching on propensity scores.

- Although weighting is generally favored among biostatisticians, many researchers suggest that it may not be an appropriate procedure when many propensity scores are very close to one or zero (e.g., Austin, 2011; Lanehart et al., 2012; Shadish & Steiner, 2010). Despite normalized and stabilized weights, overweighting may still occur. Others have demonstrated that weighting is especially sensitive to model misspecification (Freedman & Berk, 2008; Kang & Schafer, 2007), although this affects other methods as well.

- As mentioned previously, a major concern in using covariate adjustments with propensity scores is how well the assumptions are met when using an ANCOVA. This is a concern for how well not only the propensity scores meet the assumptions, but also the individual covariates. Researchers do not recommend this method when variances among covariates are heterogeneous (D'Agostino, 1998; Rubin, 2001) or when covariates or propensity scores are not linearly related to the outcome (Rosenbaum, 2010).

5.3b Propensity Score Methods Are Not a Panacea

While most researchers advocate the use of PS methods under the right conditions, it is important to know that PS methods cannot solve all of our

Figure 5.1 General guidelines for using propensity score methods

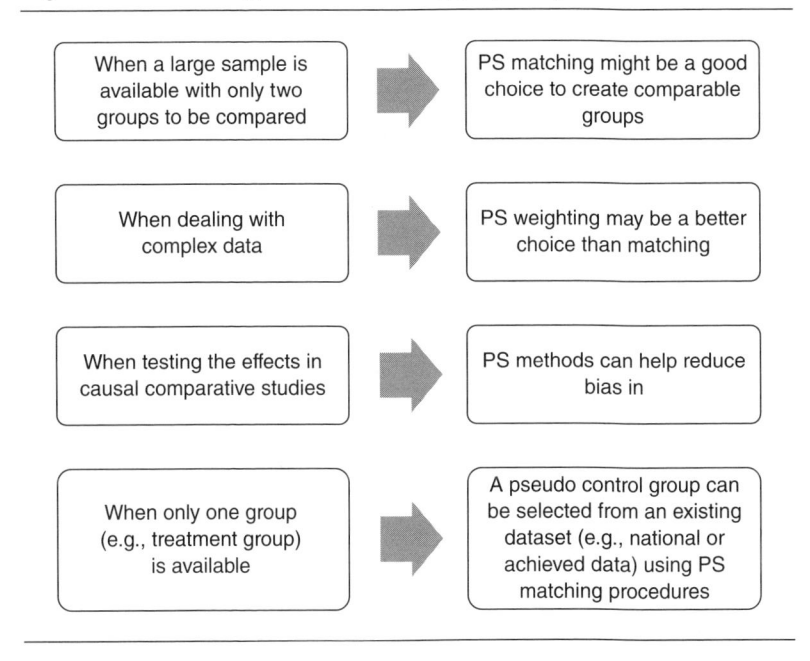

When a large sample is available with only two groups to be compared	→ PS matching might be a good choice to create comparable groups
When dealing with complex data	→ PS weighting may be a better choice than matching
When testing the effects in causal comparative studies	→ PS methods can help reduce bias in
When only one group (e.g., treatment group) is available	→ A pseudo control group can be selected from an existing dataset (e.g., national or achieved data) using PS matching procedures

research problems due to the limitations discussed in Section 5.1. We must be careful not to trust that applying PS methods will ensure that our treatment effect estimation is unbiased. PS methods can improve the accuracy of treatment effect estimates, but only when used properly and if the assumptions are met. In some specific fields, there are some guidelines (see Figure 5.1) for implementing PS methods; for example, What Works Clearinghouse (2017) for education makes several caveats to when propensity scores meet their standards, some of which we have already covered, such as (a) the covariates used in the PS model must be measured before the intervention and (b) the covariates must be balanced. Other guidelines go beyond normal PS methods procedures, such as (c) PS adjustments must be applied to pretests as well as posttest observations and (d) researchers must use a doubly robust procedure, in which both the covariates and propensity scores are included in the analytic model when estimating the treatment effects if the covariates are not balanced.

Be aware that PS methods will not sufficiently reduce bias if the propensity scores themselves are not modeled correctly (i.e., model misspecification), the assumptions of the statistical adjustment are not met, or there is not sufficient common support. Model misspecification may occur if (a) the PS model does not include all covariates that contribute to selection bias (i.e., nonignorable observations), (b) there are several missing values on the covariates used in the model, or (c) the functional form of the covariates is misspecified (i.e., covariates may need to be modeled using higher order terms). Covariate adjustment with PS can be ineffective if assumptions of an ANOVA are not met. Plausible concerns are that the propensity scores are heteroscedastic and not linearly related to the dependent variable, the variances are heterogeneous between groups, or the propensity scores may not have the same correlation with the dependent variable for each treatment group. Weighting can also be problematic when PS distributions are skewed, which is a common occurrence. While there are methods to reduce overweighting with extreme scores, they may not completely resolve the problem. Finally, poor common support often results in dropping cases (with caliper matching and subclassification) or poor matches (with greedy matching or subclassification), or it may increase the likelihood that some of the previously mentioned statistical assumptions will be violated. While dropping cases with extreme propensity scores may improve the accuracy of causal effect estimation for the limited sample of the study, it also makes it more difficult to generalize results to an intended population. One may reasonably argue that dropping cases with low propensity scores is not problematic, since these participants are unlikely to obtain the treatment. Whereas, caliper matching or trimming prior to weighting may delete cases with high propensity scores. This would be problematic, as we would want to know the treatment effects for those who are most likely to receive treatment.

5.3c Statistical Software

In previous chapters, we covered equations for estimating propensity scores, matching algorithms, and treatment effect estimation, but very few researchers actually implement PS methods by hand; most use prepackaged statistical software. While there are several statistical programs and macros that support the implementation of PS methods, any statistical package that computes a logistic regression will allow researchers to estimate the propensity scores. However, the most commonly used packages automatically compute propensity scores and match cases using one of several available PS matching algorithms. Some of these packages also estimate the adjusted treatment effects. In addition, some of these packages estimate propensity scores separately from the adjustment methods, and others allow researchers to seamlessly execute PS procedures with treatment effect estimations. Each package has its own advantages and disadvantages when running specific PS methods. Because the software, output, and options in these packages are frequently upgraded, we did not provide specific information about specific software packages in this book. However, descriptions of software packages that are popular for implementing PS methods (e.g., R, SPSS, STATA, and SAS) are provided on the book's companion website at **study.sagepub.com/researchmethods/qass/ bai&clark**. The website describes the statistical features of these programs, instructions for obtaining them, code to implement PS methods, and annotated output that interprets the results. We regularly maintain the content on the website so that the online materials are current.

5.3d Development and Trends in Propensity Score Methods

There have been several developments in PS methods over the past 20 years. While some of these are used infrequently, many have become either common or expected practices within certain fields. We do not cover all of these because this volume is an introduction to PS methods, but we would like to briefly introduce some of these methods in this section and their references.

Bootstrap PS estimation uses the average propensity scores from several bootstrap samples instead of the propensity scores from a single sample (Bai, 2013). The process consists of randomly sampling a certain number of bootstrap samples (B; e.g., $B = 200$), estimating the propensity score for each new sample (using one of the methods described in Section 2.2), and averaging the propensity scores for each case. The means of the propensity scores are used to balance the treatment groups in lieu of single-sample propensity scores. Although Bai found few differences between the single-sample and bootstrap sample propensity scores, in theory, the bootstrap estimates should be more stable.

Hierarchical PS methods are used with nested designs in which the intraclass correlation for intact groups contributes to the treatment effect (Hong & Raudenbush, 2005; Schreyögg, Stargardt, & Tiemann, 2011; Wang, 2015). Hong and Raudenbush used multilevel PS subclassification in which they created propensity scores at two levels: school (whether or not schools retain children) and student (whether or not individuals were retained in kindergarten). Propensity scores for the schools were estimated from school-level covariates, and a second set of propensity scores was estimated for the students (who attended a school that permitted retention) from student-level covariates. Both schools and students were stratified on propensity scores. Some studies use a dual matching strategy when both levels are not comparable. In practice, matching can be done just at a single level if the treatment and comparison groups are not comparable after accounting for a set of covariates only at one level (Wang, 2015).

Stabilization of weights (Harder et al., 2010; Robins et al., 2000) is a statistical adjustment made to PS weights that includes the average of the propensity scores for each treatment condition. The specific formulas are described in Section 3.2b. This type of weight is used to reduce overweighting and inflated variability caused by cases with very large or small propensity scores.

Doubly robust procedures are statistical adjustments to the treatment estimates that account for both the propensity scores and the individual covariates (Kang & Schafer, 2007; Shadish et al., 2008). These are often necessary when the PS model is misspecified. Unfortunately, we often do not know if the PS model is correct or not. To ensure that treatment estimates are unbiased, What Works Clearinghouse (2017) recommends that researchers in education always use this procedure to meet their standards for quasi-experiments. Genetic matching may be used to test for the necessity of a doubly robust procedure (Diamond & Sekhon, 2013). The *GenMatch* algorithm automatically assesses the global imbalance of all covariates and propensity scores using optimal matching. It creates weights for all covariates and the propensity scores to determine which equation will best balance the covariates. If the propensity score is correctly modeled, all other covariates will be weighted by zero. However, if the PS model is misspecified, other covariates will be weighted according to how well they can help balance the treatment groups.

Bayesian propensity score analysis (BPSA) uses Bayes's theorem in conjunction with propensity scores to account for the uncertainty of the true propensity scores (An, 2010; McCandless, Gustafson, & Austin, 2009). Traditional PS methods model propensity scores as a single, aggregated observed variable, which we assume is the true probability that a participant will be in a particular treatment condition. However, BPSA treats the propensity scores as a latent variable. Although the relationships between the outcome and the individual covariates are often considered when selecting covariates to include in a traditional PS model, the conditional distribution of the propensity scores depends on the outcome in BPSA. That is, the propensity scores are modeled based on the covariates, treatment, and outcome. Furthermore, this approach provides a more efficient analysis as it estimates the propensity scores and treatment effect simultaneously. McCandless et al. (2009) found that BPSA was especially effective when covariate imbalance was small, and An (2010) found that BPSA estimated more accurate standard errors than traditional PS methods.

REFERENCES

Abadie, A., & Imbens, G. W. (2011). Bias-corrected matching estimators for average treatment effects. *Journal of Business & Economic Statistics*, *29*, 1–11. doi:10.1198/jbes.2009.07333

Abadie, A., & Imbens, G. W. (2016). Matching on the estimated propensity score. *Econometrica*, *84*, 781–807. doi:10.3982/ECTA11293

Ahmed, A., Husain, A., Love, T. E., Gambassi, G., Dell'Italia, L. J., Francis, G. S., . . . Bourge, R. C. (2006). Heart failure, chronic diuretic use, and increase in mortality and hospitalization: An observational study using propensity score methods. *European Heart Journal*, *27*(12), 1431–1439.

Allison, P. (2012). *Logistic regression using SAS: Theory and application* (2nd ed.). Cary, NC: SAS Institute.

Almond, D. (2006). Is the 1918 influenza pandemic over? Long-term effects of in utero influenza exposure in the post-1940 U.S. population. *Journal of Political Economy*, *114*(4), 672–712.

An, W. (2010). Bayesian propensity score estimators: Incorporating uncertainties in propensity scores into causal inference. *Sociological Methodology*, *40*, 151–189.

Austin, P. C. (2009). Using the standardized difference to compare the prevalence of a binary variable between two groups in observational research. *Communications in Statistics–Simulations and Computation*, *38*, 1228–1234.

Austin, P. C. (2011). An introduction to propensity score methods for reducing the effects of confounding in observational studies. *Multivariate Behavioral Research*, *46*(1), 399–424.

Austin, P. C., & Mamdani, M. M. (2006). A comparison of propensity score methods: A casestudy estimating the effectiveness of post-AMI statin use. *Statistics in Medicine*, *25*(12), 2084–2106.

Austin, P. C., & Schuster, T. (2016). The performance of different propensity score methods for estimating absolute effects of treatments on survival outcomes: A simulation study. *Statistical Methods in Research*, *25*, 2214–2237.

Austin, P. C., & Stuart, E. A. (2015). Moving towards best practice when using inverse probability of treatment weighting (IPTW) using the propensity score to estimate causal treatment effects in observational studies. *Statistics in Medicine*, *34*, 3661–3679. doi:10.1002/sim.6607

Bai, H. (2011). Using propensity score analysis for making causal claims in research articles. *Educational Psychology Review*, *23*, 273–278. doi:10.1007/s10648-011-9164-9

Bai, H. (2013). A bootstrap procedure of propensity score estimation. *Journal of Experimental Education*, *81*, 157–177. doi:101080/00220973.2012.700497

Bai, H. (2015). Methodological considerations in implementing propensity score matching. In W. Pan & H. Bai (Eds.), *Propensity score analysis: Fundamentals, developments, and extensions*. New York: Guilford.

Baycan, I. O. (2016). The effects of exchange rate regimes on economic growth: Evidence from propensity score matching estimates. *Journal of Applied Statistics*, *43*, 914–924. doi:10.1080/02664763.2015.1080669

Bernstein, K., Park, S. Y., Hahm, S., Lee, Y. N., Seo, J. Y., & Nokes, K. M. (2016). Efficacy of a culturally tailored therapeutic intervention program for community dwelling depressed Korean American women: A non-randomized quasi-experimental design study. *Archives of Psychiatric Nursing*, *30*, 19–26. doi:10.1016/j.apnu.2015.10.011

Bowden, R. J., & Turkington, D. A. (1990). *Instrumental variables (No. 8)*. New York: Cambridge University Press.

Brookhart, M. A., Schneeweiss, S., Rothman, K. J., Glenn, R. J., Avorn, J., & Sturmer, T. (2006). Variable selection for propensity score models. *American Journal of Epidemiology, 163,* 1149–1156. doi:10.1093/aje/kwj149

Caliendo, M., & Kopeinig, S. (2008). Some practical guidance for the implementation of propensity score matching. *Journal of Economic Surveys, 22*(1), 31–72. doi:10.1111/j.1467-6419.2007.00527.x

Camillo, F., & D'Attoma, I. (2010). A new data mining approach to estimate causal effects of policy interventions. *Expert Systems With Applications, 37,* 171–181.

Clark, M. H. (2015). Propensity score adjustment methods. In W. Pan & H. Bai (Eds.), *Propensity score analysis: Fundamentals and developments* (pp. 115–140). New York: Guilford.

Clark, M. H., & Cundiff, N. L. (2011). Assessing the effectiveness of a college freshman seminar using propensity score adjustments. *Research in Higher Education, 52*(6), 616–639.

Cochran, W. G. (1968). The effectiveness of adjustment by subclassification in removing bias in observational studies. *Biometrics, 24,* 295–313. Retrieved from http://www.jstor.org/stable/2528036

Cochran, W. G., & Rubin, D. B. (1973). Controlling bias in observational studies: A review. *Sankhya, Series A, 35,* 417–446.

Cole, S. R., & Hernán, M. A. (2008). Constructing inverse probability weights for marginal structural models. *American Journal of Epidemiology, 168*(6), 656–664.

Cox, D. R. (1958). *Planning of experiments.* Oxford, UK: Wiley.

D'Agostino, R. B. (1998). Tutorial in biostatistics: Propensity score methods for bias reduction in the comparison of a treatment to a non-randomized control group. *Statistics in Medicine, 17*(19), 2265–2281.

D'Attoma, I., Camillo, F., & Clark, M. H. (2017). A comparison of bias reduction methods: Clustering versus propensity score based methods. *Journal of Experimental Education.* doi:10.1080/00220973.2017.1391161

Dehejia, R. H., & Wahba, S. (2002). Propensity score-matching methods for nonexperimental causal studies. *Review of Economics and Statistics, 84*(1), 151–161.

Diamond, A., & Sekhon, J. S. (2013). Genetic matching for estimating causal effects: A general multivariate matching method for achieving balance in observational studies. *Review of Economics and Statistics, 95,* 932–945. doi:10.1162/REST_a_00318

Duwe, G. (2015). The benefits of keeping idle hands busy: An outcome evaluation of a prisoner reentry employment program. *Crime & Delinquency, 61,* 559–586. doi:10.1177/0011128711421653

Eisenberg, D., Downs, M. F., & Golberstein, E. (2012). Effects of contact with treatment users on mental illness stigma: Evidence from university roommate assignments. *Social Science & Medicine, 75,* 1122–1127. doi:10.1016/j.socscimed.2012.05.007.

Entwisle, D. R., & Alexander, K. L. (1992). Summer setback: Race, poverty, school composition, and mathematics achievement in the first two years of school. *American Sociological Review, 57,* 72–84.

Fennema, E., & Sherman, J. (1977). Sex-related differences in mathematics achievement, spatial visualization, and affective factors. *American Educational Research Journal, 14,* 51–57.

Fillmore, K. M., Kerr, W. C., Stockwell, T., Chikritzhs, T., & Bostrom, A. (2006). Moderate alcohol use and reduced mortality risk: Systematic error in prospective studies. *Addiction Research & Theory, 14,* 101–132. doi:10.1080/16066350500497983

Freedman, D. A., & Berk, R. A. (2008). Weighting regressions by propensity scores. *Evaluation Review, 32,* 392–409. doi:10.1177/0193841X08317586

Gastwirth, J. L., Krieger, A. M., & Rosenbaum, P. R. (1998). Dual and simultaneous sensitivity analysis for matched pairs. *Biometrika, 85*(4), 907–920.

Gilbert, S. A., Grobman, W. A., Landon, M. B., Spong, C. Y., Rouse, D. J., Leveno, K. J., . . . Carpenter, M. (2012). Elective repeat cesarean delivery compared with spontaneous trial of labor after a prior cesarean delivery: A propensity score analysis. *American Journal of Obstetrics and Gynecology, 206*(4), 311.e1–311.e9.

Greenland, S. (1989). Modeling and variable selection in epidemiologic analysis. *American Journal of Public Health, 79*(3), 340–349.

Grunwald, H. E., & Mayhew, M. J. (2008). Using propensity scores for estimating causal effects: A study in the development of moral reasoning. *Research in Higher Education, 49*, 758–775. doi:10.1007/s11162-008-9103-x

Guill, K., Lüdtke, O., & Köller, O. (2017). Academic tracking is related to gains in students' intelligence over four years: Evidence from a propensity score matching study. *Learning and Instruction, 47*, 43–52. doi:10.1016/j.learninstruc.2016.10.001

Gunter, W. D., & Daly, K. (2012). Causal or spurious: Using propensity score matching to detangle the relationship between violent video games and violent behavior. *Computers in Human Behavior, 28*, 1348–1355. doi:10.1016/j.chb.2012.02.020

Guo, S., Barth, R. P., & Gibbons, C. (2006). Propensity score matching strategies for evaluating substance abuse services for child welfare clients. *Children and Youth Services Review, 28*(4), 357–383.

Guo, S. Y., & Fraser, M. W. (2015). *Propensity score analysis: Statistical methods and applications* (2nd ed.). Thousand Oaks, CA: Sage.

Gutman, L. M. (2006). How student and parent goal orientations and classroom goal structures influence the math achievement of African Americans during the high school transition. *Contemporary Educational Psychology, 31*(1), 44–63.

Hade, E. M., & Lu, B. (2013). Bias associated with using the propensity score as a regression covariate. *Statistics in Medicine, 33*, 74–87. doi:10.1002/sim.5884

Han, Y., Grogan-Kaylor, A., Delva, J., & Xie, Y. (2014). Estimating the heterogeneous relationship between peer drinking and youth alcohol consumption in Chile using propensity score stratification. *International Journal of Environmental Research in Public Health, 11*, 11879–11897. doi:10.3390/ijerph111111879

Hansen, B. B. (2004). Full matching in an observational study of coaching for the SAT. *Journal of the American Statistical Association, 99*(467), 609–618.

Hanushek, E. A., Kain, J. F., Markman, J. M., & Rivkin, S. G. (2003). Does peer ability affect student achievement? *Journal of Applied Econometrics, 18*, 527–544.

Harder, V. S., Stuart, E. A., & Anthony, J. C. (2010). Propensity score techniques and the assessment of measured covariate balance to test causal associations in psychological research. *Psychological Methods, 15*, 234–249. doi:10.1037/a0019623

Heckman, J. J. (1979). Sample selection bias as a specification error. *Econometrica, 47*, 153–161.

Heckman, J. J., Ichimura, H., Smith, J., & Todd, P. (1998). Characterizing selection bias using experimental data. *Econometrica, 66*(5), 1017–1098.

Heckman, J. J., Ichimura, H., & Todd, P. E. (1997). Matching as an econometric evaluation estimator: Evidence from evaluating a job training programme. *Review of Economic Studies, 64*(4), 605–654.

Heckman, J., & Navarro-Lozano, S. (2004). Using matching, instrumental variables, and control functions to estimate economic choice models. *Review of Economics and Statistics, 86*(1), 30–57.

Hernandez, J. C. (2000). Understanding the retention of Latino college students. *Journal of College Student Development, 41*(6), 575–588.

Hill, H., Rowan, R. B., & Ball, D. L. (2005). Effects of teachers' mathematical knowledge for teaching on student achievement. *American Educational Research Journal, 42,* 371–406.

Hirano, K., & Imbens, G. W. (2001). Estimation of causal effects using propensity score weighting: An application to data on right heart catheterization. *Health Services and Outcomes Research Methodology, 2*(3–4), 259–278.

Hirano, K., Imbens, G. W., & Ridder, G. (2003). Efficient estimation of average treatment effects using the estimated propensity score. *Econometrica, 71*(4), 1161–1189.

Ho, D. E., Imai, K., King, G., & Stuart, E. A. (2007). Matching as nonparametric preprocessing for reducing model dependence in parametric causal inference. *Political Analysis, 15,* 199–236.

Ho, D. E., Imai, K., King, G., & Stuart, E. A. (2011). MatchIt: Nonparametric preprocessing for parametric causal inference. *Journal of Statistical Software, 42*(8), 1–28.

Holland, P. W. (1986). Statistics and causal inference. *Journal of the American Statistical Association, 81*(396), 945–960. doi:10.2307/2289064

Holmes, W. M. (2014). *Using propensity scores in quasi-experimental designs.* Thousand Oaks, CA: Sage.

Hong, G., & Raudenbush, S. W. (2005). Effects of kindergarten retention policy on children's cognitive growth in reading and mathematics. *Educational Evaluation and Policy Analysis, 27*(3), 205–224.

Hosmer, D. W., & Lemeshow, S. (2000). *Applied logistic regression* (2nd ed.). Hoboken, NJ: Wiley.

Huber, M., Lechner, M., & Steinmayr, A. (2015). Radius matching on the propensity score with bias adjustment: Tuning parameters and finite sample behaviour. *Empirical Economics, 49*(1), 1–31.

Jamelske, E. (2009). Measuring the impact of a university first-year experience program on student GPA and retention. *Higher Education, 57,* 373–391. doi:10.1007/s10734-008-9161-1

Joffe, M. M., & Rosenbaum, P. R. (1999). Invited commentary: Propensity scores. *American Journal of Epidemiology, 150*(4), 327–333.

Kang, J. D. Y., & Schafer, J. L. (2007). Demystifying double robustness: A comparison of alternative strategies for estimating a population mean from incomplete data. *Statistical Science, 22,* 523–539.

Keele, L. (2010). *An overview of rbounds: An R package for Rosenbaum bounds sensitivity analysis with matched data.* White Paper, Ohio State University, Columbus, OH.

King, G., & Nielsen, R. (2016). *Why propensity scores should not be used for matching.* Retrieved from: https://gking.harvard.edu/files/gking/files/psnot.pdf

Kirchmann, H., Steyer, R., Mayer, A., Joraschky, P., Schreiber-Willnow, K., & Strauss, B. (2012). Effects of adult inpatient group psychotherapy on attachment characteristics: An observational study comparing routine care to an untreated comparison group. *Psychotherapy Research, 22,* 95–114.

Ko, T. J., Tsai, L. Y., Chu, L. C., Yeh, S. J., Leung, C., Chen, C. Y., Chou, H. C., ... Hsie, W. S. (2014). Parental smoking during pregnancy and its association with low birth weight, small for gestational age, and preterm birth offspring: A birth cohort study. *Pediatrics and Neonatology, 55,* 20–27. doi:10.1016/j.pedneo.2013.05.005

Koth, C., Bradshaw, C., & Leaf, P. (2008). A multilevel study of predictors of student perceptions of school climate: The effect of classroom-level factors. *Journal of Educational Psychology, 100,* 96–104.

Kuroki, M., & Cai, Z. (2008). Formulating tightest bounds on causal effects in studies with unmeasured confounders. *Statistics in Medicine, 27*(30), 6597–6611.

Land, K. C., & Felson, M. (1978). Sensitivity analysis of arbitrarily identified simultaneous equation models. *Sociological Methods and Research, 6,* 283–307.

Lane, K. (2002). Special report: Hispanic focus: Taking it to the next level. *Black Issues in Higher Education, 19*, 18–21.
Lanehart, R. E., De Gil, P. R., Kim, E. S., Bellara, A. P., Kromrey, J. D., & Lee, R. S. (2012, April). *Propensity score analysis and assessment of propensity score approaches using SAS procedures*. Paper presented at the SAS Global Forum, Orlando, FL.
Larzelere, R. E., & Cox, R. B. (2013). Making valid causal inferences about corrective actions by parents from longitudinal data. *Journal of Family Theory and Review, 5*, 282–299. doi:10.1111/jftr.12020
Lee, B. K., Lessler, J., & Stuart, E. A. (2010). Improving propensity score weighting using machine learning. *Statistics in Medicine, 29*, 337–346. doi:10.1002/sim3782
Lee, B. K., Lessler, J., & Stuart, E. A. (2011). Weight trimming and propensity score weighting. *PloS One, 6*(3), e18174.
Lehmann, E. L. (2006). *Nonparametrics: Statistical methods based on ranks* (Rev. ed.). New York: Springer.
Leite, W. (2017). *Practical propensity score methods using R*. Thousand Oaks, CA: Sage.
Lemon, S. C., Roy, J. R., Clark, M. A., Friedmann, P. D., & Rakowski, W. R. (2003). Classification and regression tree analysis in public health: Methodological review and comparison with logistic regression. *Annals of Behavioral Medicine, 26*, 172–181.
Leow, C., Wen, X., & Korfmacher, J. (2015). Two-year versus one-year Head Start program impact: Addressing selection bias by comparing regression modeling with propensity score analysis. *Applied Developmental Science, 19*, 31–46. doi:10.1080/10888691.2014.977995
Lewis, D. (1973). Counterfactuals and comparative possibility. *Journal of Philosophical Logic, 2*(4), 418–446.
Li, L., Shen, C. Y., Wu, A. C., & Li, X. (2011). Propensity score-based sensitivity analysis method for uncontrolled confounding. *American Journal of Epidemiology, 174*(3), 345–358.
Linden, A., & Yarnold, P. R. (2016). Combining machine learning and propensity score weighting to estimate causal effects in multivalued treatments. *Journal of Evaluation in Clinical Practice, 22*, 875–885. doi:10.1111/jep.12610
Liu, W., Kuramoto, S. J., & Stuart, E. A. (2013). An introduction to sensitivity analysis for unobserved confounding in nonexperimental prevention research. *Prevention Science, 14*(6), 570–580.
Luellen, J. K., Shadish, W. R., & Clark, M. H. (2005). Propensity scores: An introduction and experimental test. *Evaluation Review, 29*, 530–558.
Månsson, R., Joffe, M. M., Sun, W., & Hennessy, S. (2007). On the estimation and use of propensity scores in case-control and case-cohort studies. *American Journal of Epidemiology, 166*(3), 332–339.
McCaffrey, D. F., Ridgeway, G., & Morral, A. R. (2004). Propensity score estimation with boosted regression for evaluating causal effects in observational studies. *Psychological Methods, 9*(4), 403–425. doi:10.1037/1082-989X.9.4.403
McCandless, L. C., Gustafson, P., & Austin, P. C. (2009). Bayesian propensity score analysis for observational data. *Statistics in Medicine, 28*, 94–112. doi:10.1002/sim.3460
Murname, R. J., & Willett, J. B. (2011). *Methods matter: Improving causal inference in educational and social science research*. New York: Oxford University Press.
Ngai, F. W., Chan, S.W.C., & Ip, W. Y. (2009). The effects of a childbirth psychoeducation program on learned resourcefulness, maternal role competence and perinatal depression: A quasi-experiment. *Nursing Studies, 46*, 1298–1306. doi:0.1016/j.ijnurstu.2009.03.007
Nora, A. (2001). The depiction of significant others in Tinto's "Rites of Passage": A reconceptualization of the influence of family and community in the persistence process. *Journal of College Student Retention: Research, Theory & Practice, 3*(1), 41–56.

Olmos, A., & Govindasamy, P. (2015). A practical guide for using propensity score weighting in R. *Practical Assessment, Research & Evaluation, 20*. Retrieved from https://pareonline.net/pdf/v20n13.pdf

Pampel, F. C. (2000). *Logistic regression: A primer*. Thousand Oaks, CA: Sage.

Pan, W., & Bai, H. (Eds.). (2015a). *Propensity score analysis: Fundamentals and developments*. New York: Guilford.

Pan, W., & Bai, H. (2015b). Propensity score interval matching: Using bootstrap confidence intervals for accommodating estimation errors of propensity scores. *BMC Medical Research Methodology, 15*(1), 53.

Pan, W., & Bai, H. (2016). Propensity score methods in nursing research: Take advantage of them but proceed with caution. *Nursing Research, 65*(6), 421–424. doi:10.1097/NNR.0000000000000189

Pattanayak, C. W. (2015). Evaluating covariate balance. In W. Pan & H. Bai (Eds.), *Propensity score analysis: Fundamentals and developments* (pp. 89–112). New York: Guilford.

Pearl, J. (2010). The foundations of causal inference. *Sociological Methodology, 40*, 75–149. doi:10.1111/j.1467-9531.2010.01228.x

Peterson, E. D., Pollack, C. V., Roe, M. T., Parsons, L. S., Littrell, K. A., Canto, J. G., & Barron, H. V. (2003). Early use of glycoprotein IIb/IIIa inhibitors in non-ST-elevation acute myocardial infarction: Observations from the National Registry of Myocardial Infarction 4. *Journal of the American College of Cardiology, 2*, 45–53. doi:10.1016/S0735-1097(03)00514-X

Reynolds, C. L., & DesJardins, S. L. (2009). The use of matching methods in higher education research: Answering whether attendance at a 2-year institution results in differences in educational attainment. In J. C. Smart (Ed.), *Higher education: Handbook of theory and research* (pp. 47–97). New York: Springer.

Robins, J. M., Hernán, M. A., & Brumback, B. (2000). Marginal structural models and causal inference in epidemiology. *Epidemiology, 11*, 550–560.

Rosenbaum, P. R. (1989). Optimal matching for observational studies. *Journal of the American Statistical Association, 84*, 1024–1032.

Rosenbaum, P. R. (2002). Observational studies. In *Observational studies* (2nd ed., pp. 1–17). New York: Springer.

Rosenbaum, P. R. (2010). *Design of observational studies*. New York: Springer-Verlag.

Rosenbaum, P. R., & Rubin, D. B. (1983). The central role of the propensity score in observational studies for causal effects. *Biometrika, 70*, 41–55.

Rosenbaum, P. R., & Rubin, D. B. (1984). Reducing bias in observational studies using subclassification on the propensity score. *Journal of the American Statistical Association, 79*(387), 516–524.

Rosenbaum, P. R., & Rubin, D. B. (1985). Constructing a control group using multivariate matched sampling methods that incorporate the propensity score. *The American Statistician, 39*(1), 33–38.

Rothman, K. J., Greenland, S., & Lash, T. L. (1998). Types of epidemiologic studies. *Modern Epidemiology, 3*, 95–97.

Rubin, D. B. (1974). Estimating causal effects of treatments in randomized and nonrandomized studies. *Journal of Educational Psychology, 66*(5), 688–701.

Rubin, D. B. (1976). Matching methods that are equal percent bias reducing: Some examples. *Biometrics, 32*, 109–120.

Rubin, D. B. (1978). Bias reduction using Mahalanobis metric matching. *ETS Research Bulletin Series, 1978*(2), 1–10.

Rubin, D. B. (1979). Using multivariate matched sampling and regression adjustment to control bias in observational studies. *Journal of the American Statistical Association, 74*, 318–328.

Rubin, D. B. (1980). Percent bias reduction using Mahalanobis metric matching. *Biometrics*, *36*, 293–298.
Rubin, D. (1997). Estimating causal effects from large data sets using propensity scores. *Annals of Internal Medicine*, *127*, 757–763.
Rubin, D. B. (2001). Using propensity scores to help design observational studies: Application to the tobacco litigation. *Health Services and Outcomes Research Methodology*, *2*(3–4), 169–188.
Rubin, D. B. (2006). *Matched sampling for causal effects*. New York: Cambridge University Press.
Rubin, D. B., & Thomas, N. (1996). Matching using estimated propensity scores: Relating theory to practice. *Biometrics*, *52*, 249–264. doi:10.2307/2533160
Schafer, J. L., & Kang, J. (2008). Average causal effects from nonrandomized studies: A practical guide and simulated example. *Psychological Methods*, *13*(4), 279–313.
Schommer-Aitkins, M., Duell, O. K., & Hutter, R. (2005). Epistemological beliefs, mathematical problem-solving beliefs, and academic performance of middle school students. *Elementary School Journal*, *105*, 289–304.
Schreyögg, J., Stargardt, T., & Tiemann, O. (2011). Costs and quality of hospitals in different health care systems: A multi-level approach with propensity score matching. *Health Economics*, *20*(1), 85–100.
Seawright, J., & Gerring, J. (2008). Case selection techniques in case study research: A menu of qualitative and quantitative options. *Political Research Quarterly*, *61*(2), 294–308.
Sekhon, J. S. (2008). The Neyman-Rubin model of causal inference and estimation via matching methods. In J. Box-Steffensmeier, H. Brady, & D. Collier (Eds.), *The Oxford handbook of political methodology* (pp. 271–299). New York: Oxford University Press.
Setoguchi, S., Schneeweiss, S., Brookhart, M. A., Glynn, R. J., & Cook, E. F. (2008). Evaluating uses of data mining techniques in propensity score estimation: A simulation study. *Pharmacoepidemiology and Drug Safety*, *17*(6), 546–555.
Shadish, W. R. (2010). Campbell and Rubin: A primer and comparison of their approaches to causal inference in field settings. *Psychological Methods*, *15*, 3–17. doi:10.1037/a0015916
Shadish, W. R., & Clark, M. H. (2002). An introduction to propensity scores. *Metodologia de las Ciencias del Comportamiento Journal*, *4*(2), 291–298.
Shadish, W. R., Clark, M. H., & Steiner, P. M. (2008). Can nonrandomized experiments yield accurate answers? A randomized experiment comparing random to nonrandom assignment. *Journal of the American Statistical Association*, *103*, 1334–1344. doi:10.1198/0162145 08000000733
Shadish, W. R., Cook, T. D., & Campbell, D. T. (2002). *Experimental and quasi-experimental designs for generalized causal inference*. Boston: Houghton Mifflin.
Shadish, W. R., & Steiner, P. M. (2010). A primer on propensity score analysis. *Newborn and Infant Nursing Reviews*, *10*, 19–26.
Shen, C. Y., Li, X., Li, L., & Were, M. C. (2011). Sensitivity analysis for causal inference using inverse probability weighting. *Biometrical Journal*, *53*(5), 822–823.
Smith, J. A., & Todd, P. E. (2005). Does matching overcome LaLonde's critique of nonexperimental estimators? *Journal of Econometrics*, *125*, 305–353. doi:10.1016/j.jeconom.2004 .04.011
Steiner, P. M., Cook, T. D., Shadish, W. R., & Clark, M. H. (2010). The differential role of covariate selection and data analytic methods in controlling for selection bias in observational studies: Results of a within-study comparison. *Psychological Methods*, *15*, 250–267.
Stone, C. A., & Tang, Y. (2013). Comparing propensity score methods in balancing covariates and recovering impact in small sample educational program evaluations. *Practical Assessment, Research & Evaluation*, *18*(13), 1–12.

Stuart, E. A. (2010). Matching methods for causal inference: A review and a look forward. *Statistical Science: A Review Journal of the Institute of Mathematical Statistics, 25*(1), 1–21.

Stürmer, T., Joshi, M., Glynn, R. J., Avorn, J., Rothman, K. J., & Schneeweiss, S. (2006). A review of the application of propensity score methods yielded increasing use, advantages in specific settings, but not substantially different estimates compared with conventional multivariable methods. *Journal of Clinical Epidemiology, 59*, 437–447. doi:10.1016/j.jclinepi.2005.07.004

Thanh, N. X., & Rapoport, J. (2017). Health services utilization of people having and not having a regular doctor in Canada. *International Journal of Health Planning and Management, 32*(2), 180–188.

Tinto, V. (1987). *Leaving college: Rethinking the causes and cures of student attrition.* Chicago: University of Chicago Press.

Vachon, D. D., Krueger, R. F., Rogosch, F. A., & Cicchetti, D. (2015). Assessment of the harmful psychiatric and behavioral effects of different forms of child maltreatment. *Journal of American Medical Association Psychiatry, 72*, 1135–1142. doi:10.1001/jamapsychiatry.2015.1

Wang, Q. (2015). Propensity score matching on multilevel data. In W. Pan & H. Bai (Eds.), *Propensity score analysis: Fundamentals and developments* (pp. 217–235). New York: Guilford.

Weitzen, S., Lapane, K. L., Toledano, A. Y., Hume, A. L., & Mor, V. (2004). Principles for modeling propensity scores in medical research: A systematic literature review. *Pharmacoepidemiology and Drug Safety, 13*(12), 841–853.

Westreich, D., Lessler, J., & Funk, M. J. (2010). Propensity score estimation: Neural networks, support vector machines, decision trees (CART), and meta-classifiers as alternatives to logistic regression. *Journal of Clinical Epidemiology, 63*, 826–833. doi:10.1016/j.jclinepi.2009.11.020

What Works Clearinghouse. (2017). *What Works Clearinghouse standards handbook version 4.0.* Retrieved on March 3, 2018, from https://ies.ed.gov/ncee/wwc/Docs/referenceresources/wwc_standards_handbook_v4.pdf

Winship, C., & Morgan, S. L. (1999). The estimation of causal effects from observational data. *Annual Review of Sociology, 25*, 659–706.

INDEX

Analysis of covariance (ANCOVA), 8, 9, 56–57, 76, 77, 96, 99
Assignment
 appropriate conditions for using propensity scores, 12–13
 ignorable treatment assignment assumption, 13–14, 89
 nonrandom, 12–13
 random, 1, 3, 4–5
 self-selection, 1, 12
Assumptions for using propensity score methods, 13–19, 48–49, 57, 89, 98, 102
Average treatment effect (ATE), 4, 55–56, 96
Average treatment effect for the treated (ATT), 55–56, 96

Bagging, 29, 30
Balancing covariates. *See* Covariate balance
Bayesian propensity score analysis (BPSA), 104
Between-groups analysis, treatment effects estimation, 71–73, 75, 97–98
Boosted modeling, 30
Bootstrap aggregation, 29
Bootstrap propensity score estimation, 103

Caliper matching, 18, 42–43, 91–92, 95, 102
Causal comparative studies, 12–13
Causal effect estimation, 71–77. *See also* Treatment effect estimation
Causal inference, 3–9, 40
 appropriate conditions for using propensity scores, 12–13
 selection issues. *See* Assignment; Selection bias
 validity of, 5–6
Chi-square test, 33, 72, 74, 97
Classification and regression tree (CART), 26, 29, 30
Cohen's *d*, 68
Collinearity of covariates, 26

Common support, 15–19, 94–95
 checklist, 63
 graphical analysis approach, 16, 94
 inferential statistics approaches, 17–18
 maximum/minimum deletion approach, 17
 propensity score matching issues, 90, 91
 reducing problems with, 91–92
 sample size ratio matching and, 48
 summary, 94–95
 trimming approach, 17
Comparison groups, 6
Compensatory equalization, 15
Compensatory rivalry, 15
Complex matching, 45–47, 91
Confounding variables, 5
 covariate selection, 22. *See also* Covariate selection
 propensity score versus traditional covariate analyses, 24
 traditional covariate analyses and, 8, 24
 unobserved covariates, 77–79, 85, 89–90, 91. *See also* Hidden bias
Correlation analysis and covariate selection, 25, 33–35
Covariate adjustment with individual covariates, 8–11, 24
Covariate adjustment with propensity scores, 10, 56–57, 96
 appropriate use, 99
 covariate selection, 24
 statistical assumptions and, 57, 102
 traditional covariate adjustment versus, 24
 treatment effect estimation, 76
Covariate balance, 14, 65–71, 96
 evaluating selection bias, 66
 graphical approach, 70, 82, 83
 ignorable treatment assignment assumption, 14
 percent bias reduction, 70, 96
 standardized bias, 68–70, 96
 statistical check example, 80–82
 testing, 86

113

Covariate selection, 21–26, 92–94
  checklist, 37
  collinearity and overcorrection, 26
  example, 31, 33–35
  limiting hidden bias sources, 90
  mechanisms, 21–23
  procedures, 24–25, 92–94
  theoretical foundations, 23–24
Design elements
  covariate selection considerations, 25
  reducing selection bias, 6–8
Difference-in-differences
  matching, 47
Discriminate function analysis, 26
Doubly robust procedures, 76–77, 104

Ensemble methods, 26, 29–30, 94
Ethical issues in random assignment, 4
Exact matching, 40
Experimental design, 3

Factorial ANOVA, 75
Full matching, 45–46, 69, 91

Generalized linear mixed models
  (GLMMs), 74
Genetic matching, 45, 104
Graphical approach for analyzing
  common support, 16, 94
Graphical approach for assessing
  covariate balance, 70, 82, 83f
Greedy matching, 40–45, 79, 95

Hidden bias, 5, 6, 14, 77, 89–90
  sensitivity analysis, 77–79,
    84–85, 90, 98
Hierarchical linear models, 74
Hierarchical propensity score
  methods, 103
Histograms, 70, 82, 83
Hotelling's T, 71, 72, 73, 97

Ignorable treatment assignment
  assumption, 13–14, 89, 98
Independent samples
  Kolmogorov-Smirnov
  test, 17, 95
Independent samples t-test,
  71, 73, 75, 84, 97

Inferential statistics
  assessing covariate balance, 71
  common support analysis
    approaches, 17–18, 95
Instrumental variable (IV), 7, 10–11
Internal validity of observational
  studies, 5–6
Inter-University Consortium for Political
  and Social Research (ICPSR), 3, 31
Interval matching, 44
Inverse probability of treatment
  weighted (IPTW), 55, 92
Inverse probability weighting, 77

Jitter plots, 82

Kernel matching, 46–47
Kolmogorov-Smirnov tests, 17, 95

Linear programming, 77
Logistic regression, 26, 27–28,
  30, 35–37, 73, 74, 94
Love plots, 70

Machine learning, 29–30
Mahalanobis matching, 40, 44–45
Matching, 10, 39–49, 57–58, 95
  assessing covariate balance.
    See Covariate balance
  caliper, 18, 42–43, 91–92, 95, 102
  common support analysis
    approaches, 18, 48–49
  common support issues, 90, 91
  complex, 45–47, 91
  exact, 40
  example, 58–63
  full, 45–46, 69, 91
  genetic, 45, 104
  greedy, 40–45, 79, 95
  Mahalanobis, 40, 44–45
  nearest neighbor, 40, 42, 58–60
  on multiple covariates, 11
  optimal, 45, 91
  outliers and, 62
  potential problems with, 90–91
  proximal, 8
  quasi-experimental designs
    and, 7–8
  ratio, 48, 62, 69
  statistical software packages, 58

subclassification or stratification, 49–54
hierarchical methods, 103
summary, 95
treatment effect estimation after, 71–74, 82, 84, 96–97
typology, 31, 39–40
without replacement, 42, 47–48, 92
with replacement, 42, 47–48, 91
Maximum likelihood approach, 27
McNemar's test, 73, 97
Metaclassification, 30
Model misspecification, 76, 99, 101–102, 104
propensity score weighting issues, 92
traditional covariate analyses and, 8
Multinomial logistic regression, 72
Multiple covariates, matching on, 11
Multiple regression, 8, 56–57, 76, 96, 99
Multivariate analysis of variance (MANOVA), 72, 74

Natural experiments, 12–13
Nearest neighbor matching, 40, 42, 58–60
Neural networks, 26
Normalized weights, 75, 98, 100

Observational studies, 1
causal inference, 3–9, 40
internal validity of, 5–6
reasons for using propensity scores, 10–11
selection bias. *See* Selection bias
when to use propensity scores, 12–13
Observed covariates, 6, 10, 13–14, 27, 65, 84, 89
One-way analysis of variance (ANOVA), 72, 79
Optimal matching, 45, 91
Outlier effects, 62
Overcorrection of covariates, 26

Paired samples *t*-test, 71, 73, 97
Percent bias reduction (PBR), 70, 96
Placebos, 6
Playworks data, 21, 31–33
Pretests, 6–7
Propensity score adjustment methods, 95–96
covariate adjustment, 10, 56–57, 96

hierarchical methods, 103
matching, 39–49, 57–58, 95
subclassification or stratification, 10, 49–54, 95–96
weighting, 10, 54–56, 96
See also Covariate adjustment with propensity scores; Matching; Subclassification; Weighting
Propensity score estimation
models, 26–30, 94
bootstrap, 103
example, 31, 35–37
summary, 94
Propensity score matching. *See* Matching
Propensity score methods, 39, 56–57
advantages over other methods, 10–11
applications, 2
appropriate use, 12–13, 19–20, 99
assumptions, 13–19, 48–49, 57, 89, 98
Bayesian propensity score analysis, 104
checklist for using, 19–20
development and trends, 103–104
effectiveness considerations, 99
example, 58–63
hierarchical methods, 103
rationale for using, 1
summary of procedures, 92–98
See also Propensity score adjustment methods
Propensity score methods, limitations and issues, 11, 89, 99–102
appropriate conditions, 12–13
common support, 91–92
ignorable treatment assignment assumption, 13–14, 89
propensity score matching, 90–91
sample reduction or exclusion, 91–92
stable unit treatment value assumption, 14–15
unobserved covariates, 89–90. *See also* Hidden bias
weighting, 92, 102
See also Common support; Hidden bias; Model misspecification
Propensity scores, 9–10, 37
adjustment methods. *See* Propensity score adjustment methods
common support across treatment and control groups. *See* Common support

estimation models, 26–30
reasons for using, 10–11
weighting using inverse of, 55.
   See also Weighting
when to use, 12–13, 19–20
Propensity score weighting.
   See Weighting
Proximal matching, 8

Q-Q plots, 70, 82
Quasi-experimental designs, 7–8, 104

Radius matching, 44
Random forests, 29
Randomized control trials (RCTs), 4, 13
Random selection or assignment, 1
   experimental design, 3
   feasibility issues, 4–5
Ratio matching, 48, 62, 69
Regression discontinuity design (RDD), 13
Repeated measures MANOVA, 73
Resentful demoralization, 15
Rosenbaum's bound, 77–79, 84–85, 98

Sample size, common
   support problems and, 91
Sample size ratio matching, 48, 62
Selection bias, 1, 5, 65
   advantages of using propensity
      scores, 10–11
   checking covariate balance, 66
   confounding variables and, 5–6
   existing methods for reducing, 6–9
   testing covariate balance.
      See Covariate balance
   traditional covariate
      analyses and, 8–9
   unobserved covariates. *See* Hidden bias
Self-selection, 1, 12
Sensitivity analysis, 77–79, 84–85, 90, 98
Simultaneous sensitivity analysis, 78
Stabilized weights, 75, 98, 100, 104
Stable unit treatment value assumption
   (SUTVA), 14–15
Standardized bias (SB), 68–70, 96
Standardized mean difference,
   18, 68, 93, 94–95
Standard mean difference, 18
Statistical software packages,
   58, 102–103

Stratification (subclassification),
   10, 18, 49–54
Subclassification, 10
Subclassification (stratification),
   18, 49–54, 95–96
   common support, 95
   summary, 95–96
   treatment effect estimation
      after, 74–75

Testing for covariate balance.
   See Covariate balance
Treatment and control group common
   support or overlap.
   See Common support
Treatment conditions and covariate
   selection, 22–23. *See also*
   Covariate selection
Treatment diffusion, 15
Treatment effect, 4
   covariate selection mechanisms, 22–23.
   See also Covariate adjustment
      with propensity scores
   stable unit treatment value
      assumption, 14–15
   weighting procedures for
      finding, 55–56
Treatment effect estimation
   after matching, 71–74, 82,
      84, 96–97
   after subclassification, 74–75, 97
   ANCOVA, 76, 77.
      See also Analysis of covariance
   average treatment effect (ATE),
      4, 55–56, 96
   average treatment effect for the treated
      (ATT), 55–56, 96
   chi-square test of association, 72, 74
   covariate adjustment, 76
   doubly robust procedures, 76–77, 104
   example, 82, 84
   factorial analysis of variance, 75
   generalized linear mixed models, 74
   hierarchical linear models, 74
   independent samples *t*-test,
      71, 73, 75, 84, 97
   McNemar's test, 73, 97
   multinomial logistic regression, 72
   multiple regression, 76. *See also*
      Multiple regression

multivariate ANOVA, 72, 74
one-way ANOVA, 72, 79
paired samples t-test, 71, 73, 97
propensity score weighting,
    75–76, 98
repeated measures ANOVA or
    MANOVA, 73
sensitivity analysis, 77–79, 84–85
Tree-based methods, 26, 28–29, 30, 94
t-tests, 33, 71, 72, 73, 75, 76, 82, 84, 97
Two-factor analysis of variance
    (ANOVA), 74–75, 97
Two-sample Kolmogorov-Smirnov test, 71

Unobserved or unmeasured covariates,
    77–79, 85, 89–90, 91.
    See also Hidden bias
Unreliability of treatment
    implementation, 15

Validity of statistical causal
    inference, 5–6, 15

Weighting, 10, 54–56, 96
    appropriate use, 99
    assessing covariate balance, 68–69
    inverse probability of treatment
        weighted, 55, 92
    normalized, 75, 98, 100, 104
    stabilized weights, 75, 98, 100, 104
    potential problems with, 92, 99, 102
    stabilization of weights, 104
    treatment effect estimation,
        75–76, 98
What Works Clearinghouse, 101, 104
Wilcoxon's Signed Rank statistic, 78, 84
Wilks' lambda, 72, 73
Within-groups analysis, treatment
    effects estimation, 71–74, 97